Army

Logistics:

Issue and Sale of Personal Clothing

22 July 2014

United States Government
US Army

UNCLASSIFIED

SUMMARY of CHANGE

AR 700-84
Issue and Sale of Personal Clothing

This major revision, dated 22 July 2014--

o Compiles responsibilities for Clothing and Services Office and Headquarters, Department of the Army, U.S. Army Tank-Automotive and Armaments Command Life Cycle Management Command, under U.S. Army Materiel Command (para 1-4*c*).

o Introduces the capability to initiate DA Form 3078 (Personal Clothing Request) via an online Web-based system versus the current manual system (para 1-6*p*).

o Revises initial issue duffel bag marking instructions (para 1-7).

o Updates example of completed DA Form 3078 with instructions to be in line with FY 14 Clothing Bag (fig 3-1).

o Adds an example DD Form 139 (Pay Adjustment Authorization) with instructions (fig 3-2).

o Revises the Exchange mail-order procedures to Web-based procedures and provides new telephone numbers for service (para 3-12).

o Changes Army Blue Uniform to Army Service Uniform under reference to allowances (para 4-8).

o Adds gratuitous issue of clothing bag items for medical evacuees (para 5-4*k*).

o Adds Army direct ordering as a program established to provide sustainment of clothing bag items (funded by Military Personnel Army funds) to Soldiers in combat operations (para 5-4*m*).

o Revises list for what commanders of Army National Guard and U.S. Army Reserve Soldiers who enlist more than 60 days before initial active duty for training can elect to issue (para 5-6*b*).

o Clarifies policy for Army National Guard and U.S. Army Reserve Soldiers attending initial active duty for training report with all previously issued uniforms. (para 5-6*d*).

o Gives the Commander, U.S. Army Cadet Command responsibility to establish policies and procedures pertaining to preventing inventory excess, ensuring Cadet insignia, awards, badges and decorations are not in contravention with existing law or policy, and to assist the Deputy Chief of Staff, G-1 with estimation of commutation rates (para 10-8*d*).

o Adds new policy for Wounded Warrior Clothing Support Program (paras 13-5, 13-6, and 13-7).

o Authorizes the U.S. Army Reserve to use the Central Clothing Distribution Facility to provide issue-in-kind clothing (para 14-1).

o Adds requirements for U.S. Army Reserve recruiters to ensure all Soldiers are completely in-processed with the unit prior to going to schools, and to allow for ample time for issue of uniform (para 14-6*b*).

o Changes references to Army Green Uniform to Army Service Uniform (throughout).

Headquarters
Department of the Army
Washington, DC
22 July 2014

*Army Regulation 700–84

Effective 22 August 2014

Logistics

Issue and Sale of Personal Clothing

By Order of the Secretary of the Army:

RAYMOND T. ODIERNO
General, United States Army
Chief of Staff

Official:

GERALD B. O'KEEFE
Administrative Assistant to the
Secretary of the Army

History. This publication is a major revision.

Summary. This regulation covers the issue and sale of personal clothing in the Army.

Applicability. This regulation applies to the Active Army, the Army National Guard/Army National Guard of the United States, and the U.S. Army Reserve, unless otherwise stated.

Proponent and exception authority. The proponent of this regulation is the Deputy Chief of Staff, G–4. The proponent has the authority to approve exceptions or waivers to this regulation that are consistent with controlling law and regulations. The proponent may delegate this approval authority, in writing, to a division chief within the proponent agency or its direct reporting unit or field operating agency in the grade of colonel or the civilian equivalent. Activities may request a waiver to this regulation by providing justification that includes a full analysis of the expected benefits and must include formal review by the activity's senior legal officer. All waiver requests will be endorsed by the commander or senior leader of the requesting activity and forwarded through higher headquarters to the policy proponent. Refer to AR 25–30 for specific guidance.

Army internal control process. This regulation contains internal control provisions in accordance with AR 11–2 and identifies key internal controls that must be evaluated (see appendix B).

Supplementation. Supplementation of this regulation and establishment of command and local forms are prohibited without the prior approval from the Deputy Chief of Staff, G–4 (DALO–SUI), Washington, DC 20310–0500.

Suggested improvements. Users are invited to send comments and suggested improvements on DA Form 2028 (Recommended Changes to Publications and Blank Forms) directly to the Office of the Deputy Chief of Staff, G–4 (DALO–SUI), 500 Army Pentagon, Washington, DC 20310–0500.

Distribution. This publication is available in electronic media only and is intended for command levels C, D, and E for Active Army, Army National Guard/Army National Guard of the United States, and the U.S. Army Reserve.

Contents (Listed by paragraph and page number)

Chapter 1
Introduction, *page 1*

Section I
General, page 1
Purpose • 1–1, *page 1*
References • 1–2, *page 1*
Explanation of abbreviations and terms • 1–3, *page 1*

Section II
Responsibilities, page 1
Responsibilities • 1–4, *page 1*
Authority • 1–5, *page 4*
General provisions • 1–6, *page 4*
Identification marking • 1–7, *page 5*

---

*This regulation supersedes AR 700–84, 18 November 2004.

Contents—Continued

Chapter 2
Army Military Clothing Store, *page 6*
Introduction • 2–1, *page 6*
Establishment and disestablishment of Army military clothing store • 2–2, *page 6*
Display of clothing items • 2–3, *page 6*
Customer service • 2–4, *page 6*
Fitting uniforms • 2–5, *page 7*
Quality control • 2–6, *page 7*
Inventory of personal and organizational clothing • 2–7, *page 7*
Cross-service support agreements • 2–8, *page 7*

Chapter 3
Sales Procedures, *page 8*
Authorized patrons • 3–1, *page 8*
Identification of patrons • 3–2, *page 9*
General limitations on sales • 3–3, *page 9*
Pricing • 3–4, *page 10*
Exchange on sales • 3–5, *page 10*
Sales • 3–6, *page 10*
Civilian purchase of utility uniform • 3–7, *page 11*
Purchase of uniforms for members of other Services participating in Joint command exercises • 3–8, *page 11*
Uniform Clothing Deferred Payment Plan through use of the Military Star Card • 3–9, *page 11*
Individual charge sales (payroll deduction) to enlisted Soldiers on active duty • 3–10, *page 11*
Processing individual charge sales (payroll deduction) • 3–11, *page 12*
Internet sales or sales through the Exchange call center • 3–12, *page 15*
Sale of defective, soiled, or damaged Defense Logistics Agency-Troop Support merchandise • 3–13, *page 15*
Reporting shipping and packaging discrepancies • 3–14, *page 15*
Price reductions • 3–15, *page 15*
Transfer of Condition Code B clothing • 3–16, *page 16*

Chapter 4
Allowances Under the Clothing Monetary Allowance System, *page 16*
Initial allowances of personal clothing • 4–1, *page 16*
Personnel entitled to initial allowances • 4–2, *page 17*
Clothing monetary allowance or clothing replacement allowance • 4–3, *page 17*
Increase in authorized allowances • 4–4, *page 18*
Replacement of initial allowances with new items • 4–5, *page 18*
Supplemental clothing allowance • 4–6, *page 18*
Supplemental allowance authorization • 4–7, *page 18*
Army Service uniform payment and accounting • 4–8, *page 18*
Maternity uniform • 4–9, *page 19*
Clothing and footwear for Soldiers allergic to fabric, dye, or metal • 4–10, *page 19*

Chapter 5
Personal Clothing Issue Procedures, *page 19*
Obtaining personal clothing items • 5–1, *page 19*
Issue of items to enlisted Soldiers during initial processing • 5–2, *page 20*
Issue of personal clothing items during other than initial processing • 5–3, *page 22*
Gratuitous issue • 5–4, *page 22*
Issue and attachment of insignia • 5–5, *page 25*
Reserve Component Soldiers ordered to initial active duty for training • 5–6, *page 25*
Reserve Component Soldiers ordered to extended active duty • 5–7, *page 26*
Clothing for prisoners in Army confinement facility • 5–8, *page 26*
Initial issue to prisoners restored to duty • 5–9, *page 28*
Clothing for prisoners detained in personnel control facilities • 5–10, *page 28*

Contents—Continued

Exchange or alteration of misfit clothing and footwear • 5–11, *page 29*
Exchanges of clothing for reasons other than misfit • 5–12, *page 29*
Initial and gratuitous issues to Soldiers isolated from supporting installations • 5–13, *page 30*
Nonpay status • 5–14, *page 30*
Reenlistments • 5–15, *page 30*

Chapter 6
Clothing Initial Issue Point, *page 30*
Introduction • 6–1, *page 30*
Concept of operations • 6–2, *page 30*
Establishment • 6–3, *page 31*
Inventories • 6–4, *page 31*
Inventory and operations • 6–5, *page 31*
Physical layout and processing • 6–6, *page 31*
Alteration facilities • 6–7, *page 32*

Chapter 7
Special Measurement Clothing and Footwear, *page 32*
Special measurement clothing • 7–1, *page 32*
Procedures for supply of special measurement clothing • 7–2, *page 32*
Special measurement footwear • 7–3, *page 33*
Procedures for supply of special measurement footwear • 7–4, *page 33*
Prices of special measurement clothing and footwear • 7–5, *page 34*
Supply of orthopedic footwear • 7–6, *page 34*

Chapter 8
Civilian Clothing, *page 34*
Introduction • 8–1, *page 34*
Who may receive allowances • 8–2, *page 34*
Who may approve allowances • 8–3, *page 37*
Types and quantities of allowances • 8–4, *page 37*
Procedures for requesting allowances • 8–5, *page 38*
Procedures for receiving clothing allowance • 8–6, *page 39*

Chapter 9
Supply of Individual Clothing for Senior and Junior Reserve Officers' Training Corps, *page 39*
Purchase limitations • 9–1, *page 39*
Limitations of issue • 9–2, *page 40*
Conservation of uniform clothing • 9–3, *page 40*
Requisitioning channels • 9–4, *page 40*
Requisitioning procedures • 9–5, *page 40*
Measuring instructions • 9–6, *page 41*
Supply of individual clothing through commutation of uniform allowance • 9–7, *page 41*
Purchase of individual clothing items from Army stocks • 9–8, *page 41*
Issue and sale of footwear and purchase of personal clothing items • 9–9, *page 41*
Accounting for clothing • 9–10, *page 42*
Storage of clothing at the end of the school year • 9–11, *page 43*
Financial liability investigation of property • 9–12, *page 43*

Chapter 10
Commutation of Uniforms for Reserve Officers' Training Corps Activities, *page 43*
Introduction • 10–1, *page 43*
Requesting commutation funds • 10–2, *page 44*
Restrictions on payments • 10–3, *page 44*
Payments of funds • 10–4, *page 44*

Contents—Continued

Authorized activities • 10–5, *page 44*
Disposing of uniforms • 10–6, *page 44*
Uniform commutation rates • 10–7, *page 44*
Functions • 10–8, *page 44*
Eligibility for uniform commutation funds • 10–9, *page 45*
How to obtain uniform commutation funds • 10–10, *page 45*
Inactivation or change in system • 10–11, *page 45*
Transfer of basic and advanced course enrolled members • 10–12, *page 46*

Chapter 11
Transfer of Enlisted Soldiers on Active Duty, *page 46*
Losing command • 11–1, *page 46*
Gaining command • 11–2, *page 46*
Clearance from clothing repair, Army military clothing stores, and alteration facilities • 11–3, *page 46*

Chapter 12
Retention and Disposition of Clothing, *page 47*
Introduction • 12–1, *page 47*
Personnel with more than 3 years active duty • 12–2, *page 48*
Personnel with 3 years or fewer active duty • 12–3, *page 48*
Personnel with 6 months (180 days) or less active duty service • 12–4, *page 48*
Soldiers of the Reserve Components on initial active duty for training • 12–5, *page 48*
Soldiers of the Reserve Components who transfer from Reserve Components to Active Army • 12–6, *page 49*
Personnel being discharged or separated for medical reasons • 12–7, *page 49*
Personnel accepting a commission or warrant officer appointment • 12–8, *page 49*
Personnel discharged under bad conduct or dishonorable conditions • 12–9, *page 49*
Personal clothing receipt statement • 12–10, *page 50*
Nonretention of clothing • 12–11, *page 51*
Clothing items not authorized for retention • 12–12, *page 51*
Clothing of absentees • 12–13, *page 51*
Clothing of enlisted Soldiers dropped from the rolls • 12–14, *page 51*
Clothing of hospitalized personnel • 12–15, *page 52*
Clothing of enlisted personnel on ordinary or emergency leave, temporary duty, or pass • 12–16, *page 53*
Abandoned and unclaimed clothing in laundries and dry-cleaning plants • 12–17, *page 53*
Unclaimed repaired or altered clothing left in Government or commercial facilities • 12–18, *page 53*
Deceased personnel • 12–19, *page 54*

Chapter 13
Alterations, *page 54*
Alterations at government expense • 13–1, *page 54*
Alterations at enlisted Soldier's expense • 13–2, *page 54*
Facilities available to officers and warrant officers • 13–3, *page 54*
Authorized alterations • 13–4, *page 54*
Wounded Warrior Clothing Support Program for U.S. Army Medical Command Wounded Warrior transition units • 13–5, *page 55*
Wounded Warrior Clothing Support Program clothing modification and alterations procedures • 13–6, *page 56*
Wounded Warrior Clothing Support Program alterations criteria • 13–7, *page 56*
Unauthorized alterations • 13–8, *page 56*

Chapter 14
Issue-In-Kind System for U.S. Army Reserve Personal Clothing, *page 56*

Section I
U.S. Army Reserve Central Clothing Distribution Facility, page 56
Extension of central clothing distribution facility • 14–1, *page 56*

Contents—Continued

Mission • 14–2, *page 56*

Section II
Central Clothing Distribution Facility, page 57
Inventories • 14–3, *page 57*
Sale of clothing by the central clothing distribution facility • 14–4, *page 57*

Section II
Issue-in-Kind for U.S. Army Reserve Personal Clothing, page 57
Introduction • 14–5, *page 57*
Requests for personal clothing • 14–6, *page 60*
Inventory of personal clothing upon receipt • 14–7, *page 60*
Army Reserve Soldiers ordered to annual training or service schools • 14–8, *page 60*
Accounting for personal clothing • 14–9, *page 61*
Accounting for personal clothing when Soldiers are released from initial active duty for training • 14–10, *page 61*
Accounting for personal clothing when members are released from active duty with a reserve contractual obligation • 14–11, *page 62*
Accounting for personal clothing on change of status • 14–12, *page 62*
Processing turn-ins of personal clothing • 14–13, *page 62*
Personal clothing for U.S. Army Reserve Soldiers departing for 30 days or more of active duty for operational support • 14–14, *page 63*
Personal clothing for U.S. Army Reserve individual ready reserve Soldiers • 14–15, *page 63*
Issue-in-kind for individual ready reserve or individual mobilization augmentation Soldiers • 14–16, *page 63*
Active Guard Reserve and Active Component Soldiers assigned to troop program units • 14–17, *page 64*
Unauthorized alterations • 14–18, *page 64*
Authorized alterations • 14–19, *page 64*
Clothing for Soldiers enrolled in the Reserve Officers' Training Corps Simultaneous Membership Program • 14–20, *page 64*
Exchange or replacement of personal clothing for U.S. Army Reserve troop program unit Soldiers • 14–21, *page 65*

Chapter 15
Clothing Support to the Army National Guard, *page 65*

Section I
Army National Guard Central Clothing Distribution Facility, page 65
Establishment • 15–1, *page 65*
Mission • 15–2, *page 65*
Inventories • 15–3, *page 65*
Sale of clothing by the central clothing distribution facility • 15–4, *page 66*

Section II
Issue-in-Kind for Army National Guard Personal Clothing, page 66
Introduction • 15–5, *page 66*
Requests for personal clothing • 15–6, *page 66*
Army National Guard personnel attending annual training, Army area school, or Army service schools other than initial activity duty for training • 15–7, *page 67*
Accounting for personal clothing • 15–8, *page 67*
Accounting for personal clothing on change of status • 15–9, *page 68*
Turn-ins • 15–10, *page 68*
Exchange or replacement of personal clothing • 15–11, *page 68*
Optional exchange procedures for personal clothing • 15–12, *page 69*

Chapter 16
Evaluations and Inspections, *page 69*
Deputy Chief of Staff, G–4 • 16–1, *page 69*
Evaluations • 16–2, *page 69*

Contents—Continued

Internal controls • 16–3, *page 69*
Purpose • 16–4, *page 69*

Appendixes

A. References, *page 70*

B. Internal Control Evaluation, *page 75*

Table List

Table 1–1: Statement by corporals through sergeants major (active component), *page 4*
Table 1–2: Statement by corporals through sergeants major (reserve component), *page 4*
Table 5–1: Gratuitous issue of specified clothing bag items, *page 23*
Table 5–2: Medal of honor recipient authorization, *page 24*
Table 5–3: Clothing requirement for prisoners in Army correctional or confinement facilities, *page 27*
Table 5–4: Clothing required for prisoners in Army correctional and/or confinement facilities, pretrial and/or casual confinement status (temporary issue), *page 28*
Table 8–1: Authorized points of contacts at Army command level, *page 35*
Table 10–1: Institutions qualifying and approved for commutation, *page 43*
Table 12–1: Retention of personal clothing items for Soldiers transferred to U.S. Army Reserve control groups, *page 47*
Table 12–2: Statement of personal clothing receipt, *page 51*
Table 12–3: Clothing statement for enlisted Soldiers with a remaining reserve obligation, *page 51*
Table 12–3: Statement of personal clothing belonging to person transferred to a medical detachment, *page 53*
Table 12–4: Statement of shipment of clothing, *page 53*
Table 13–1: Authorized alterations for men's uniforms, *page 55*
Table 13–2: Authorized alterations to women's uniforms, *page 55*

Figure List

Figure 3–1: Example of a completed DA Form 3078, *page 13*
Figure 3–2: Example of a completed DD Form 139, *page 14*
Figure 5–1: Example of a completed DA Form 7000, *page 21*
Figure 14–1: Example of a completed DA Form 4886, *page 58*
Figure 14–1: Example of a completed DA Form 4886–continued, *page 59*

Glossary

Chapter 1
Introduction

Section I
General

1-1. Purpose
This regulation prescribes the policies, procedures and responsibilities for the issue and sale of personal clothing to members of Army activities and to Department of the Army civilians (DACs). It also describes systems for the maintenance, replacement, and disposition of such clothing and gives conditions under which these systems apply. Policies and procedures in this regulation are designed specifically for enlisted Soldiers (Active Army, Army National Guard (ARNG) and U.S. Army Reserve (USAR)), although limited policies or procedures may apply to officers, warrant officers, Reserve Officers' Training Corps (ROTC), Army Senior Reserve Officers' Training Corps (SROTC), Junior Reserve Officers' Training Corps (JROTC), DACs, and ROTC contracted employees. Additionally, it applies to other personnel or organizations supported under the clothing replacement allowance (CRA) or issue-in-kind systems, or Army Military Clothing Store (AMCS) operated by the Exchange.

1-2. References
Required and related publications and prescribed and referenced forms are listed in appendix A.

1-3. Explanation of abbreviations and terms
Abbreviations and special terms used in this regulation are explained in the glossary.

Section II
Responsibilities

1-4. Responsibilities
a. The Deputy Chief of Staff, G-4. The DCS, G-4 will—

(1) Assist Army commanders, Exchange, and the Superintendent, U.S. Military Academy by making periodic inspections to AMCS to ensure that business operations are in compliance with established policies and procedures.

(2) Develop and approve policies and procedures for the Army clothing program.

(3) Monitoring the overall operation of the clothing monetary allowance (CMA) system.

(4) Coordinate with Headquarters, the Exchange regarding operation of AMCS.

(5) Chair the Army uniform board.

(6) Participate in or represent the Army at Office of the Secretary of Defense (OSD), Defense Logistics Agency (DLA), or Joint Service meetings involving clothing matters.

(7) Participate in periodic reviews of material obligations with DLA-Troop Support (DLA-TS) inventory managers.

b. The Director/Chief Executive Officer, Exchange. The Director/CEO, Exchange will—

(1) Operate AMCS according to memorandums of agreement (MOAs) and policies established in Army regulations (ARs).

(2) Maintain direct contact with Headquarters, Department of the Army (HQDA), Clothing and Services Office (CSO), and Army commands (ACOMs).

(3) Report monthly the dollar value of DLA-TS inventory on hand to the CSO (AMSTA-LCS-PSC), E-5027 Blackhawk Road, Aberdeen Proving Ground, MD 21010-5424.

(4) Submit monthly electronic billings for operating costs incurred in the operation of worldwide AMCS to the CSO (AMSTA-LCS-PSC), E-5027 Blackhawk Road, Aberdeen Proving Ground, MD 21010-5424 and to U.S. Army Tank-Automotive and Armaments Command (TACOM), Integrated Logistics Support Center, Business Management Directorate (AMSTA-LCB-F/Building 45, Room L-117) 15 Kansas Street, Natick, MA 01760-1553. Billings will be broken out by installation and cover the period being billed.

c. Commander, U.S. Army Materiel Command. The Commander, AMC (U.S. Army TACOM, CSO) will—

(1) Assist ACOMs, Army service component commands (ASCCs), the Exchange, and the Superintendent, U.S. Military Academy by making periodic management assistance visits to AMCSs and clothing initial issue points (CIIPs) to ensure compliance with established policies and procedures.

(a) Recommend corrective action when needed to improve the services provided, inventory of items, or appearance of the facilities.

(b) Function as the Army focal point for Exchange inquiries on policies, concepts, interpretations, methods, and systems concerning the Army clothing program.

(c) Participate in periodic reviews of material obligations with DLA-TS inventory managers.

(d) Process suggestions concerning the Army clothing program.

(e) Maintain records, obtain data, and develop reports, studies, and projects when requested by the DCS, G–4 (DALO–SUI).

(f) Budget for, and reimburse, the Exchange for DLA–TS related operating costs incurred in the operation of AMCS.

(g) Program, budget, and manage AMC Army Working Capital Fund requirements for clothing items in AMCS.

(h) Budget for operation and maintenance, Army (OMA) funds for subsequent facility upgrade.

(2) In concert with the Director of Clothing and Heraldry and Chief, CSO, ensure that the supporting Defense accounting officer pays the Exchange for all properly documented noncash transactions made by the AMCS.

d. Commander, U.S. Army Reserve and Chief, National Guard Bureau. The Commander, USAR and CNGB will—

(1) Establish procedural guidance for operation of a USAR and ARNG central clothing distribution (CCD).

(2) Disseminate CCD policy and procedural guidance in the form of a National Guard CCD Management Plan (http://www.ngmmc.com/gmmc_news/downloads.asp) and a CCD User Handbook (http://www.ngmmc.com/downloads/UserHandBook.pdf). Users of the CCD for USAR and ARNG will use the following Web site: http://www.kyloc.com.

e. Commanders of Army commands, Army service component commands, and direct reporting units. Commanders, ACOMs, ASCCs, and DRUs will—

(1) Designate appropriate staff elements for communication with HQ Exchange and CSO.

(2) Recommend policy or procedure changes to improve AMCS operations.

(3) Budget and fund for the upgrade of a facility required by relocation of an existing AMCS to an Exchange co-located facility.

(4) Conduct unannounced spot checks of AMCS and secure technical assistance from the CSO or chief of the applicable exchange region, when necessary.

(5) Provide CSO with information and recommended solutions to any problems that cannot be resolved at installation or ACOM levels.

(6) Ensure compliance with AR 210–20.

f. Installation commanders. Installation commanders in the Active Army will—

(1) Evaluate the responsiveness of AMCS service to customer needs and command requirements.

(2) Provide suitable buildings for operating the AMCS in accordance with the installation master plan. Ensure that additional facilities requirements comply with the installation master plan, in that existing assets are being effectively and efficiently used, thereby justifying the need prior to initiating a new project.

(3) Together with the installation AMCS manager, determine the requirements for the establishment and disestablishment of AMCS and annexes and the hours of operation for maximum customer service and economy of operation.

(4) Ensure compliance with this regulation by all personnel and unit commanders under their jurisdiction.

(5) Conduct spot checks of AMCS when considered necessary and secure technical assistance from the CSO, ACOM, or chief of the applicable Exchange AMCS region when necessary.

(6) Designate in writing an officer (or civilian) in charge of the CIIP if this activity is operated at the installation.

(7) Take corrective action on inspections and reports of inspections pertaining to their area of responsibility.

(8) Ensure that persons are properly processed on transfer, so far as allowances, serviceability, appearance, and fit of clothing are concerned.

(9) Budget and fund for the upgrade of a facility required by relocation of an existing AMCS. The DCS, G–4 will approve relocations of AMCS and the installation will fund the relocation. Notify the Commander, TACOM Life Cycle Management Command, (CSO and Integrated Logistics Support Center, Business Management Office Building 45, Room 143, AMSTA–LC–W–BA, Natick, MA 01760–1553) of all upgrades and renovations.

(10) Together with the AMCS manager, and with written approval of the Exchange commander and CSO, select merchandise designated as organizational clothing and individual equipment (OCIE) and authorize for inventory in the AMCS.

(11) Inform the AMCS manager of any planned field training exercises and increases or decreases of student loads that would increase or decrease demands.

(12) Ensure that test uniforms, footwear, and related items shipped to the installation are delivered and tested within the rules established by the Army activity conducting the test program. Ensure that evaluation reports are submitted by testing individuals to the designated addressee.

(13) Staff the CIIP with sufficient personnel to perform functions efficiently.

g. Unit commanders. The commanders will—

(1) Exercise caution to assure only personal clothing items listed in common table of allowance (CTA) 50–900 (available at the Force Management Web site: https://webtaads.belvoir.army.mil) are entered on Department of the Army (DA) Form 3078 (Personal Clothing Request).

(2) Maintain control on individual charge sales and keeps the approval of such sales to a minimum per paragraph 3–10.

(3) Ensure the duffel bag is properly marked per paragraph 1–7.

(4) Direct the inspection and inventory of personal clothing at least annually, as indicated below. The record of inspection and inventory will be recorded on DA Form 3078, for active component Soldiers, or DA Form 4886 (Issue-In-Kind Personal Clothing Record), for reserve component Soldiers. However, commanders may permit corporals through sergeants major to furnish a statement that all their clothing and items are serviceable (as shown in table 1–1 for active component Soldiers and table 1–2 for reserve component Soldiers). Commanders may conduct inspections and inventories more frequently if they wish. Only keep the most recent inspection and inventory result on file. Clothing inspection and inventory will be conducted—

(a) On completion of 6 months (180 days) of active duty service, per paragraph 5–2*b*(4)(b).

(b) On arrival of newly assigned personnel per paragraph 11–2.

(c) At duty station on return from outside continental United States (OCONUS).

(d) Prior to departure of personnel for OCONUS movement or other permanent change of stations, per paragraph 11–1.

(e) Prior to departure and immediately upon return of personnel from attendance at Service schools.

(f) At the discretion of the unit commander, except as stated in paragraphs 1–4*g*(4)(a) through 1–4*g*(4)(e).

(5) Ensure enlisted Soldiers under their command obtain the following allowances:

(a) Initial allowances of personal clothing items during initial processing. Only new DLA–TS procured clothing items will be issued to new recruits.

(b) Required supplementary allowances of personal clothing, if applicable, as approved by the DCS, G–4 (see paras 4–6 and 4–7).

(6) Ensure authorized items of personal clothing are in the possession of individuals and that clothing is kept serviceable at all times.

(7) Ensure initial allowance of personal clothing items sold in AMCS is properly fitted and, if required, altered at the time of issue or sale.

(8) Ensure sale, issue, and alteration facilities are provided, as required.

(9) Ensure uniforms are properly fitted in accordance with TM 10–227 and AR 670–1.

(10) Ensure clothing is worn, as prescribed.

(11) Ensure Soldiers understand they are not required to purchase items in excess of authorized allowances.

(12) Ensure personnel are aware of the prohibition to sell, gift, loan, barter, or pledge clothing to unauthorized persons. Further, it is unauthorized to obtain any clothing from the Defense Reutilization and Marketing Service (DRMS) to exchange for serviceable items.

h. Finance officers. The officers will start the necessary action for payment of authorized monetary allowance, stoppage of such payment, and collections against pay for individual charge sales.

i. Enlisted Soldiers. The Soldiers will—

(1) Have in their possession, in a serviceable condition at all times, the items and quantities of personal uniform clothing for which they are provided a CRA to maintain. This includes requirements for new and supplemental allowances per paragraphs 4–5 and 4–6.

(2) Maintain a smart military appearance at all times. Make sure their uniforms fit properly and are worn in a military manner.

(3) Active Army enlisted Soldiers use CRA to replace clothing bag (CB) items. The enlisted Soldier is responsible for accumulating the allowance to purchase CB items authorized by CTA 50–900. The CRA is not applicable to ARNG or USAR enlisted Soldiers on active duty fewer than 179 days, as they receive issue-in-kind items from the CCD system.

(4) Safeguard their uniforms and equipment at all times, including during all movements, unless military authority directs movement of baggage on a unit basis or on a Government bill of lading.

(5) Assure that distinctive or common items of the uniform purchased from commercial sources are certified commercial by the project manager, Soldier protection and individual equipment (PM SPIE) and meet the specification for the like design, shade, cloth, and fit of the military item.

Table 1–1
Statement by corporals through sergeants major (active component)

I....(Name and Rank)...., have in my possession all items of personal clothing issued to me on DA Form 3078. All items are in the authorized quantities, serviceable, and meet the fitting and appearance standards in accordance with AR 670–1 and TM 10–227.

(Signature, Rank, and Date)
Note: Soldiers' will replace shortages and unserviceable items at their expense.

Table 1–2
Statement by corporals through sergeants major (reserve component)

I....(Name and Rank)...., have in my possession all items of personal clothing issued to me on DA Form 4886. All items are in the authorized quantities, serviceable, and meet the fitting and appearance standards in accordance with AR 670–1 and TM 10–227.

(Signature, Rank, and Date)

Note: Soldiers will replace shortages at their expense. Items found to be unserviceable due to fair wear and tear (FWT) will be turned-in and replacements requested.

1–5. Authority

a. Statutory authority.

(1) Section 4562, Title 10, United States Code (10 USC 4562) authorizes the President to prescribe the quantity and kind of clothing furnished to Service members.

(2) 37 USC 418 also authorizes the President to prescribe the amount of cash allowance to be paid to enlisted Soldiers when clothing is not furnished.

(3) 10 USC 4621 authorizes the sale of clothing.

(4) 5 USC 5901 authorizes amount of cash to be provided civilians for the purchase of an approved DA uniform and footwear, when required for wear during field exercises conducted by the military.

(5) 10 USC 772 authorizes the wear of the uniform by retirees, select former Soldiers and select civilians.

b. Delegation of authority. By Executive Order 10113, the President delegated the functions vested in 37 USC 418 to the Secretary of Defense. On April 18, 2008, the Office of the Under Secretary of Defense further delegated authority to the Assistant Secretary of the Army (Acquisitions, Logistics and Technology) (ASA (ALT)).

1–6. General provisions

a. Regardless of the system or method used to furnish enlisted Soldiers with individual clothing, nothing in this regulation will prohibit the recovery of clothing when it is in the best interest of the Government to do so when directed by HQDA. This regulation will not restrict the Army in exercising control over personal clothing.

b. Any departure from provisions of the clothing allowance system will require prior approval from the ASA (ALT).

c. The mission of the AMCS is to provide DLA–TS clothing and make cash and individual charge sales.

d. Clothing and footwear items will be fitted by trained fitters in accordance with TM 10–227. At the time of issue or sale, outer garments and footwear must be tried on while wearing the proper subgarments. The fit of clothing items must be inspected by trained fitters. Individuals will not be advised or permitted to accept a poorly fitted garment or footwear. If items are to be exchanged at the next duty station or at a later date, the clothing record will be annotated as such by the fitter. Clothing purchased from the CCD is not permitted to be exchanged at the AMCS for the correct size.

e. Articles of outer personal clothing (Army service uniform (ASU) items, Army combat uniforms (ACUs), coat or trousers, and all-weather coats) issued as part of the initial allowance or purchased by enlisted Soldiers from AMCS will be altered, if required, to fit the individual at time of issue or purchase.

(1) During the first 6 months (180 days) of active duty service.

(a) The government will incur the cost of alterations to outer clothing made during the first 6 months of service or through completion of initial entry training (IET), whichever occurs last. Replacement is authorized from the AMCS when physical profile changes during the first 6 months (180 days) of service are such that the cost of alterations to items of outer individual clothing would exceed the cost of replacement (cost of replacement less reissue or resale value of replaced items). First priority of issue will be made from stocks of serviceable Condition Code B used clothing. The AMCS manager will decide whether replacement is more economical than alteration. Commanders will authorize the exchange or alteration by processing enlisted Soldiers through the CIIP or AMCS (see para 5–11).

(b) Whenever possible, the U.S. Army Training and Doctrine Command (TRADOC) CIIP will exchange misfit clothing and footwear for IET Soldiers prior to their departure for their next duty station. Soldiers clothing and footwear will be in accordance with AR 670–1 and TM 10–227.

(c) Soldiers may exchange misfit footwear within 90 days of initial issue. Commanders will authorize the exchange of footwear by processing enlisted Soldiers through the CIIP or AMCS (see para 5–11).

(2) After the first 6 months (180 days) of service, except at the time of issue or sale, alteration to personal clothing will be at the expense of the Soldier.

f. Repairs to individual clothing and footwear after the first 6 months (180 days) of initial issue or after 90 days of service will be at the expense of the Soldier.

g. The Secretary of the Army may exempt certain areas from providing a clothing allowance system. In exempted areas, replace personal clothing worn out through FWT through the issue-in-kind system. Under such a system, except in combat areas, the Soldier will incur the costs for dry cleaning, pressing, or laundering. Government or contractual laundry and dry cleaning facilities will be made available for this purpose, except in the ARNG and USAR. In combat areas (field laundry only) dry cleaning, pressing, or laundering will be at Government expense. These services will be either through necessary processing of items and return to wearer or through exchange of soiled for clean items. Personal clothing and individual equipment of enlisted Soldiers on the clothing issue-in-kind system will be repaired or altered at Government expense.

h. When a person cannot be fitted properly from stock sizes (tariff) or by alterations, a requisition for special measurement clothing will be submitted per paragraph 7–2.

i. Special measurement footwear will be requisitioned when required per paragraph 7–3.

j. Clothing and footwear for personnel allergic to fabric, dye, or metal will be submitted, when required, per paragraph 4–10.

k. Orthopedic footwear will be provided as a medical appliance under the following conditions:

(1) The normal criteria for furnishing medical appliances to military Soldiers must be met per paragraph 7–6.

(2) Footwear must be manufactured using a special orthopedic.

(3) The enlisted Soldier requesting orthopedic alterations to standard footwear at Government expense must furnish the footwear.

l. Policy for the issue or sale of personal clothing to ROTC cadets and institutions is in chapters 9 and 10.

m. Basic policies covering the condition, appearance, and serviceability standards of clothing are in TM 10–8400–201–23. The CIIP priority for issue of new service and utility uniforms and the AMCS priority for the issue and sale of new and used service and utility uniforms is as follows (to include misfit exchanges):

(1) Issue priority is as follows:

(a) First. Limited or substitute standard Condition Code "B" (used) 75 percent remaining wear, fully serviceable and meets the standards of appearance.

(b) Second. Limited or substitute standard Condition Code "A" (new).

(2) Sale priority is as follows:

(a) First. Standard Condition Code B (used) 75 percent remaining wear, fully serviceable, and meets standards of appearance (color variance is authorized).

(b) Second. Standard Condition Code A (new).

(2) Sale priority is as follows:

(a) First. Condition Code A (new).

(b) Second. Condition Code B (used), 75 percent remaining wear.

(3) Condition Code A and Condition Code B items are authorized for issue or sale in AMCS.

(4) Only new leather footwear is authorized for issue or sale in AMCS and at CIIP.

n. AMCS will maintain DA Form 7000 (Delegation of Authority - Army Military Clothing Stores) for all commissioned officers authorized to approve or sign requests for noncash transactions on DA Form 3078. See figure 5–1 for an example DA Form 7000.

o. The CIIP will maintain DA Form 1687 (Notice of Delegation of Authority-Receipt for Supplies). See DA Pamphlet (DA Pam) 710–2–1 for guidance on the form.

p. The procedures for submitting the DA Form 3078 are below:

(1) Unit supply personnel prepare the DA Form 3078 on a Government-issued computer via the Army Publishing Directorate Web site and forward the form electronically to the unit commander for approval.

(2) Unit commanders will approve the DA Form 3078 in accordance with paragraph 1–4*g*(1) and will forward it electronically to the CSO (https://da3078.natick.army.mil; individual account needed).

(3) After approval from the CSO, the system will auto-generate an e-mail notification to the supply sergeant or specialist to pick up the requested item at the nearest AMCS.

(4) In the event of a net-centric failure or power outage, a hard copy DA Form 3078 is authorized.

(5) Regardless of method, appropriate completion of the form, as well as proper documentation, as appropriate, are required. A sample of a completed DA Form 3078 with instructions is at figure 3–1.

1–7. Identification marking

a. Permanent marking is not authorized. The initial issue duffel bag identification marking will be placed in the end plastic pocket (9 1/8 X 6 1/2) to display rank, Soldier's last name, first name, and middle initial, the last four numbers of their social security number (SSN), and unit assignment (typed or hand written). If the reception center makes the issue, the commander makes certain that markings are properly applied before the Soldier is transferred to another unit. The mark "US" is applied at the time an item is procured. The unit commander is not concerned with this marking except to renew a faded or blurred mark.

b. Applies to OCONUS shipment and when the Soldier is under OCONUS movement orders.

Chapter 2
Army Military Clothing Store

2–1. Introduction
This chapter provides policies and procedures for AMCS. Procedures maybe modified, if necessary, to adapt to automation.

2–2. Establishment and disestablishment of Army military clothing store
a. The CSO may establish an AMCS at installations with 300 or more active duty Army personnel, or disestablish where fewer than 300 active duty Army personnel are assigned. The installation commander will request to establish or disestablish an AMCS, after coordination with the installation Exchange manager, through the ACOM to the CSO (AMSTA–LC–SPS), E-5027 Blackhawk Road, Aberdeen Proving Ground, MD 21010–5424, for approval by the CSO and the Exchange. ACOMs must provide funds for initial upgrade or movement and estimated annual sales of DLA–TS garments.

b. Nation Guard installations or USAR centers are not authorized an AMCS.

2–3. Display of clothing items
a. Displays that are neat and attractive create a modern retail atmosphere. Types of displays vary from one AMCS to another; however, design displays with the customer in mind. Information and display signs will be in good taste and professional in appearance and workmanship. Prominently display prices of clothing items stocked in AMCS.

b. Install large mirrors in selected locations to enable the clerk cashier to observe any part of the AMCS which otherwise might be obscured by clothing display cases. The AMCS will contain readily accessible dressing rooms and mirrors for patron's use. This will permit the try on method of fitting.

c. Displayed merchandise will be readily accessible with sizes and prices visible. Display shirts, drawers, and socks by size. Adjust lighting to give the best effect on displayed items.

d. Steam or press ASU coats, trousers, slacks, and skirts for sale or issue that are not free of wrinkles before placing on display racks.

e. Properly fit garments displayed on mannequins or forms.

f. If necessary, clean, steam, press, or reclassify shopworn garments. Protect items displayed on open shelves and open racks to prevent deterioration.

g. Separate Condition Code B, 75 percent wear items (used) from new items. Properly tag these items for ready identification as serviceable clothing. Remove all rank insignia from serviceable used clothing items offered for sale or issue. If obvious discoloration is noticeable after removal of the insignia, reclassify the item and transfer to the DRMS. For medical reasons, the AMCS will not accept dirty or soiled serviceable used items.

h. Unpack and hang clothing items on racks in a standby area or warehouse to allow wrinkles to diminish before hanging them in the AMCS.

i. Attach sizes of uniform items to the sleeve of the coat or on trousers or skirts by clips or other methods. This will aid the customer in finding the correct size, minimize handling, and maintain stocks in the proper place.

j. Use of wooden hangers improves the appearance of military uniform items.

2–4. Customer service
a. Evaluate complaints of unsatisfactory merchandise with the intent of improving customer satisfaction.

b. The very latest equipment installed in a new AMCS located in the center of community activity, with an adequate inventory, can function properly only if responsible personnel are assigned. Clothing AMCS personnel must always present a neat appearance. They must have a friendly attitude toward all customers.

c. The AMCS operating hours will provide optimum shopping time for supported personnel. Operating hours similar to other personal service activities are most advantageous. Prominently display store hours outside the AMCS building on a sign indicating there is an AMCS located there. Inform customers well in advance of any change to operating hours. This is particularly important if the AMCS intends to close at times such as holidays or for inventories. The installation daily bulletin is a good source to announce this information. The AMCS will always be opened at the published times and patrons welcomed to enter the AMCS up to the published closing time. All AMCS personnel and managers will strive to provide maximum customer service.

d. Furnish information on item shortages to the patrons as a courtesy. Consider the use of appropriately worded signs within the AMCS denoting shortages and soliciting customer understanding.

e. When alterations to clothing at Government expense are authorized, expeditious processing will prevent inconvenience to the customer. Free alteration is authorized to enlisted Soldiers for DLA–TS items. Alteration slips will reflect that officers are not permitted free alterations on DLA–TS items. Desired service time will be 1 to 4 days. When alterations at Government expense are completed, press coats and trousers that are not wrinkle free. Locate the alteration facility close to the AMCS for customer convenience. Commercial sources with alteration contracts will establish pickup and delivery schedules convenient to the AMCS and customer.

2–5. Fitting uniforms

a. The Army requires a high standard of dress and appearance for all personnel. To maintain this high standard, AMCS must ensure that garments are free of defects, are available, and are properly fitted to the Soldier at the time of the sale or issue. A properly fitted uniform gives the Soldier the feeling of being well dressed, creates high morale, and presents a smart military appearance. Except for mail order purchases, uniforms will not be sold or issued until they have been tried on and checked by trained clothing fitters for the best fit from regular tariff sizes. This is very important since garments of a given size may vary and all persons have different physical features. Only by actually trying on each outer garment can it be determined that the approved fit has been achieved.

b. Individuals who purchase or are issued sized Army Service Uniform outer items will be informed of DA policy for fitting uniforms and footwear. This will prevent complaints from Soldiers who claim they were not fitted properly at some other installation.

c. Commanders will not require (and will discourage) all persons from making unauthorized alterations. This includes unit commanders and commanders or commandants of service schools, officer candidate schools, noncommissioned officer schools, and academies. Garments that have undergone unauthorized alterations, such as form fitting, pegging, or tapering, are not accepted for turn-in, exchange, or reissue. Replacement of these garments will be at the expense of the individual.

2–6. Quality control

To maintain a high standard of quality, managers must report all deficiencies found in clothing items during inspection. Managers will notify the CSO on any deficiency and request submission of Standard Form (SF) 368 (Product Quality Deficiency Report (PQDR)) electronically at http://www.gsa.gov/portal/forms/type/SF.

2–7. Inventory of personal and organizational clothing

a. Maintain reasonable availability (for sale or issue) of clothing items and accouterments designated as personal clothing for male and female personnel. Requisition items not in inventory because of exceptionally low demands from DLA–TS on a special order basis (excluding OCIE). Do not stock items not meeting Army specifications (commercially procured) without authorization from the DCS, G–4 (DALO–SUI).

b. The AMCS may stock a selection of merchandise designated as OCIE (see CTA 50–900). If the installation or community commander desires to stock OCIE in AMCS, the selection of items will be a joint effort of the commander and the AMCS manager. Only stock items stocked by the installation central issue facility (CIF). Coordinate the selection of items for inventory with the installation CIF. The Exchange manager and the CSO will approve the list of selected OCIE items. If there is not a CIF on the installation, the DCS, G–4 (DALO–SUI) will approve the list of selected OCIE items. Request for approval must contain items and the estimated dollar value of initial inventory of OCIE. Maintain a copy of the approved list in the AMCS. The sale of OCIE is to permit replacement of lost, damaged, or destroyed property for which the individual is financially liable. All OCIE purchased at AMCS, regardless of who pays for it, always remains Government property. This includes OCIE maintained at educational institutions that host ROTC programs and all OCIE or Government property that was issued to them in support of the ROTC program in accordance with AR 710–2. OCIE items available for sale are not intended to be used to duplicate sets of OCIE for displays or inspections, or to be used for other than Government-related missions. Inventory of OCIE in AMCS is not intended for personal use such as camping or scout activities.

c. OCIE is not for sale to local nationals. Unit commanders may authorize foreign students to purchase replacement items lost, damaged or destroyed for which an individual is liable. Commanders will provide a letter to the AMCS authorizing the foreign student to purchase the OCIE.

d. AMCS procures personal clothing and OCIE items from DLA–TS based on a memorandum of understanding between DLA–TS and the Exchange. These items are included in Federal Stock Classes 7210 and 8305 through 8475. The AMCS will not stock military occupational specialty (MOS) specific items.

2–8. Cross-service support agreements

a. The local Exchange or AMCS management will coordinate with the installation commander and the CSO to initiate or terminate cross-service support agreements for AMCS support for requiring activities. AMCS management will establish a cross-service support agreement in writing to stock other Services (non-Army) DLA—TS items.

b. If the host installation has members of another military Service assigned, the local AMCS probably has a bona fide requirement to offer the sale of uniform clothing or accouterments, unique to the other (tenant) Service. The level of support provided will vary depending on the items requested, number and types of tenant personnel assigned, physical space available, and the alternative means to support (special order, mail order, or online catalog).

(1) The other Service commander must validate their requirements by submitting a formal memorandum through the AMCS to the host commander, who endorses back "approved or disapproved" to the Exchange manager, who sends these documents to the Exchange headquarters for review; the CSO grants final approval.

(2) The request should state how many personnel (officer and enlisted) require support. Attach a list of the requested military clothing items. The CSO will only consider items with a genuine need. Once coordination is complete, the AMCS will maintain a file copy for review by inspectors and higher headquarters.

Chapter 3
Sales Procedures

3–1. Authorized patrons
Individuals listed below may purchase clothing and individual equipment items authorized for wear and use by the individual purchaser, subject to limitations in this regulation.

a. Officers, warrant officers, and enlisted Soldiers of the Active Army, Navy, Air Force, Marine Corps, and Coast Guard on active and retired lists.

b. Officers, warrant officers, and enlisted Soldiers of the Reserve Components (RCs) of the Armed Forces on active duty, retired, or granted retirement pay because of physical disability.

c. Officers, warrant officers, and enlisted Soldiers of the RCs of the Armed Forces who—

(1) Are not on active duty while in a Reserve pay status.

(2) Are not in a Reserve pay status; however, they are required to wear the uniform while employed by the RCs for participating in training assemblies or have orders for active duty training.

d. Red Cross uniformed personnel. American National Red Cross Service Program and Army utilization personnel (see AR 930–5).

e. Civilians assigned to OCONUS commands and contract surgeons of the Armed Forces who are authorized or required to wear the uniform.

f. Cadets of the U.S. Military Academy.

g. Foreign military personnel receiving training in the United States (see AR 12–15). A letter or statement from the allied training officer showing student's name, items, and quantities authorized will be presented to AMCS at the time of purchase.

h. Foreign military personnel assigned to accredited military attaches and missions.

i. Commissioned officers of the Public Health Service on active duty, retired, or granted retirement pay because of physical disability.

j. DA Civilians and Exchange associates required to wear DLA–TS items during field exercises conducted by the military. These personnel are authorized to purchase such items from the AMCS at Government expense. Commanders are authorized to use the Government purchase card. Proper identification, along with a commander's statement listing clothing items required and quantities requested, will be presented to AMCS at time of sale (see para 3–7 for procedures). Insignia, for DACs, as shown in AR 670–1, will be attached and worn on the civilian uniform. Insignia will be obtained through normal supply channels.

k. Army ROTC cadets and faculty members of institutions hosting Army cadets (see para 9–1c). The professor of military science (PMS) will authorize the purchase by memorandum listing the names of faculty members and cadets to the AMCS manager. All sales will be at no cost to the Government.

l. Department of Defense (DOD) contractors from the Armed Forces Radio and Television Service. These personnel are authorized to purchase uniform items from AMCS for producing television spot announcements.

m. Select former Soldiers who served honorably in time of war (declared or undeclared), whose most recent discharge from the Army was under honorable conditions (see para 3–3k for procedures). These personnel are not permitted to purchase the ACU in accordance with AR 670–1 and 10 USC 772.

n. A family member, acting as the agent for a military member on active duty for more than 30 days. These persons may purchase items from the AMCS. However, the purchase must be for use by the military member. The designated family member must present Department of Defense (DD) Form 1173 (Uniformed Services Identification and Privilege Card) and attest (with a letter or verbal statement) that the purchased items are for use by the military member.

3–2. Identification of patrons

a. Persons purchasing or receiving issues of clothing and equipment from AMCS must establish their identity as authorized customers. Identification will be made by presenting a valid Armed Forces identification card or DAC identification card, as appropriate.

b. Identification on mail order sales is required for the following:

(1) Soldiers on active duty and retired personnel will create and submit a statement attesting to their duty status (active duty or retired).

(2) Soldiers in Reserve status, not on active duty, will create and submit a request through their reserve unit headquarters for endorsement. In the absence of a unit commander, the unit advisor or the custodian of records may endorse the request. Information required in the endorsement is as follows

(a) Status of the person submitting the request.

(b) A statement that the person is serving in a reserve pay status.

(3) Enlisted Soldiers of RCs on active duty must present a copy of their orders that placed them in an active duty status.

(4) For a consolidated order for several purchasers, a statement to this effect must be submitted with the order, as well as the names of all the purchasers.

3–3. General limitations on sales

a. Sale of the uniform and distinctive parts of the uniform is restricted to members of the Army unless otherwise authorized by law, in accordance with AR 670–1 and 10 USC 771.

b. Sales to prospective enlisted graduates of officer candidate schools will be made as follows:

(1) Before making the sale, the officer candidate must present to the AMCS manager a statement of qualification signed by the school commandant or an authorized representative. The statement must indicate that the officer candidate is qualified and is expected to graduate.

(2) Items of officer clothing and insignia prescribed for graduation exercises and additional items required for wear after graduation and commissioning may be fitted, altered, and sold for cash, or they may be set aside up to 4 weeks before graduation for sale after graduation and commissioning.

(3) Candidates who fail to graduate do not have to pay for alterations or for garments that have been set aside. If uniforms set aside for sale after commissioning are not purchased because a candidate failed to graduate, the AMCS will—

(a) Return unaltered garments to stock.

(b) Sell altered garments to other authorized purchasers, if possible.

(4) Candidates successfully completing the course are required to purchase any uniforms set aside for sale after graduation.

c. Distinctive items of the Army uniform will not be sold to officers or enlisted members of other military departments or to foreign military personnel (see AR 670–1 for clothing listed as distinctive).

d. Distinctive officer uniform and identification devices will be sold to enlisted Soldiers only if they are Reserve officers on inactive duty or are officer candidates.

e. Sales may be made to Red Cross personnel, civilians assigned to OCONUS commands, and civilian faculty members of ROTC institutions hosting senior ROTC cadets.

f. Sales to officers, warrant officers, and enlisted Soldiers of the RCs of the armed forces on active duty will be limited to items of the uniform authorized for wear in performing their military duty.

g. Sales to officers and warrant officers of the RC not on active duty will be limited to uniform items necessary for wear in performing their military duty. Enlisted Soldiers not on active duty are only permitted to buy nonrecoverable items not exceeding authorized allowances.

h. The DCS, G–4 and Army commanders, as delegated, may restrict or suspend sales of certain items to ensure supply support to persons on active duty.

i. Sales to retired members of the Armed Forces are limited to service, dress, and mess uniforms (including accessories), footwear, physical fitness uniforms and undergarments. See AR 670–1 for policy on wear of ASUs and accessories by retired personnel.

j. Army retired personnel serving as JROTC instructors are authorized to purchase required clothing items, including the ACU and accessories for themselves. Purchases will be at no expense to the Government. The brigade or region headquarters (Active or RCs) commander will authorize the purchase by memorandum to the AMCS manager.

k. Disabled American Veterans honorably discharged from the Army on 100 percent disability, who can provide proof of that disability, are entitled to purchase Army Service Uniforms (including accessories) footwear and undergarments. See AR 670–1 for policy on wear of ASUs and accessories.

l. Select former Soldiers who served honorably in time of war (declared or undeclared), whose most recent discharge from the Army was under honorable conditions, can purchase specific uniform items authorized for active duty personnel from the AMCS.

(1) Periods of war or campaigns, declared and undeclared, are defined in AR 600–8–22.

(2) This authorization is restricted to purchase of specific uniform items (service, mess uniforms, optional dress uniforms) and accessory items (headgear, insignia, medals, and ribbons) required for wear during specific occasions in accordance with 10 USC 772 and AR 670–1.

(3) All other select former Soldiers who have an honorable discharge or have been discharged from the Army under honorable conditions may purchase insignia, medals, and ribbons for display purposes. Additional medals may be purchased for wear with civilian clothing as permitted by AR 670–1.

(4) This policy does not apply in areas where international agreements prohibit the use of AMCS by retirees and select former Soldiers.

(5) This authorization does not include utility uniforms, accessories items, ACUs, boots, and items commonly available from commercial sources, such as black socks, white underwear, handkerchiefs, and black dress shoes.

(6) Purchaser must first obtain permission from the installation commander or their representative to gain access to the installation, if necessary, and to the AMCS for the purpose of purchasing uniforms or accessory items.

(7) The commander or their representative will determine the purchaser's intended use of the items and will advise the purchaser of the current wear policy in accordance with AR 670–1.

(8) At the time of purchase, the purchaser must present to the AMCS representative proof of honorable discharge or discharge under honorable conditions and any other identification that may be required by the installation commander. For convenience, the DD Form 214 (Certification of Release or Discharge from Active Duty), copy number four, may be photocopied, reduced, and laminated at the purchaser's expense.

3–4. Pricing

a. Clothing and footwear prices are contained in the Department of Defense – Electronic Mall (DOD EMALL). The AMCS will—

(1) Issue or sell special measurement clothing and footwear to enlisted Soldier using the DOD EMALL standard prices.

(2) Sell special measurement clothing and footwear to officers using the DOD EMALL standard prices.

(3) Sell Condition Code B clothing (75 percent wear) at 50 percent of the DOD EMALL price.

(4) Sell special measurement clothing items at the current price for tariff sizes of like items.

b. The installation commander will annually set and approve prices for contract operations performing alterations. Prices will be at the amount best representing the total cost of the service. Collections for services will be credited as appropriation reimbursement.

3–5. Exchange on sales

a. The exchange of a DLA–TS garment or AMCS item is permitted, if the item is in the same condition as it was at the time of sale and purchased from the AMCS. Proof of purchase (cash register receipt) must be presented.

b. AMCS will not exchange a worn item because of improper fit regardless of date of sale.

c. Handle DLA–TS items with defects in workmanship or material as follows:

(1) There is no time limit for returning defective DLA–TS items to an AMCS so long as the defect is validated by the AMCS manager.

(a) All defective DLA–TS items returned without a receipt must have a valid DLA–TS contract number in the inside tag. Items without the tag or DLA contract number will not be accepted for return.

(b) The AMCS will not accept defective item purchased from an Army surplus store or commercial enterprise.

(2) The AMCS will authorize repairs of the DLA–Troop Support item at government expense if economical to repair and if the repairs would not cause a visible defect.

(3) The AMCS will exchange returned non-repairable DLA–TS items. The AMCS manager will follow guidelines set forth in paragraph 2–6. Exchange of the ACU because of color or shade variances between trousers and coats is not authorized. These variances are expected after washing or cleaning.

3–6. Sales

a. Payment may be made with cash, personal credit card, personal check, certified check, travelers check, fund cite, or money order made payable to the Exchange. AMCS managers will not—

(1) Accept checks from persons if there is doubt the check can be collected.

(2) Accept postdated checks.

(3) Cash checks as a matter of convenience.

(4) Accept personal checks for amounts exceeding the purchase price unless it falls within the check cashing policies of the Exchange.

(5) Accept two-party checks needing an endorsement.

b. When a cash register is used, all cash sales will be registered at the time of sale. The AMCS manager or a representative other than the cashier will verify cash sales daily. Only these two people will have access to the cash register tape.

c. Cash refunds for returned merchandise are authorized. Cash refunds are made only if the item returned is in a new and unused condition. The customer must show proof of purchase from AMCS.

3–7. Civilian purchase of utility uniform
a. Commanders may authorize OMA funds, through use of the government purchase card, for the purchase of civilian uniforms, undershirts, footwear, and other uniform-related items. Nametapes, nameplates, and insignia will be furnished and attached at Government expense.

b. Personnel who are emergency essential and on signed mobility agreements will retain clothing while assigned within the program.

c. Upon termination of requirements, recoverable items will be turned in to the individual's supporting activity.

3–8. Purchase of uniforms for members of other Services participating in Joint command exercises
a. ACOMs supporting Joint command exercises may not authorize the purchase of the ACU. Footwear for members of other Services may be authorized to participate in field exercises.

b. Joint command agencies will provide OMA funds. The Joint commander or their representative will sign a statement to verify request.

c. Commanders will not request, and the AMCS will not issue, clothing to any individual required to purchase the clothing or to have it in their possession.

d. Upon reassignment, the individual will turn-in recoverable clothing to the supporting unit. Recoverable clothing will remain Government property.

e. The supporting unit will establish a clothing pool of recoverable items to support the Joint agency.

f. Uniforms will be hand receipted to the individuals on DA Form 3645–1 (Additional Organizational Clothing and Individual Equipment Record).

g. The individual will retain issued nonrecoverable items.

3–9. Uniform Clothing Deferred Payment Plan through use of the Military Star Card
In accordance with procedures established by the Director/CEO, Exchange, the AMCS will provide a Uniform Clothing Deferred Payment Plan (UCDPP) for the sale of uniforms, uniform accessories, and footwear.

3–10. Individual charge sales (payroll deduction) to enlisted Soldiers on active duty
Unit commanders will initiate individual charge sales (payroll deduction) only for Soldiers in a pay status and with no fewer than 60 active duty days before the Soldier's scheduled discharge or separation date.

a. Individual charge sales (payroll deduction) are authorized to cover emergency needs of an enlisted Soldier who is without funds to purchase essential clothing items needed for health and welfare. The requirement to make up shortages for an inspection is not considered an emergency, nor will individual charge sales be authorized if the Soldier can wait until regular pay and allowance is received.

b. Valid emergency needs that could contribute to an individual being without funds are—

(1) Fire or theft of clothing.

(2) Return to military control from unauthorized absence.

(3) Release from confinement to duty.

(4) Undue delay in receipt of pay and allowances.

(5) Loss of personal funds.

(6) Qualified compassionate reasons.

c. Individual charge sales are not authorized for—

(1) Soldiers in a nonpay status or Soldiers with 60 days or fewer of active duty before separation of discharge. Place in the remarks block of DA Form 3078 the date of the Soldier's separation or discharge. If the Soldier is in an undetermined confinement status or has been ordered to a confinement or correctional facility, the date of departure from the installation must also be stated. If the Soldier is not in a pay status or has fewer than 60 days before discharge or separation, the unit commander will apply, through supply channels, for a temporary issue of used serviceable recoverable items.

(2) Organizational clothing and individual equipment items.

(3) Purchase of commercial items.

d. All individual charge sales will be charged to the enlisted Soldier's military personnel, Army (MPA) appropriation for payment.

e. When an enlisted Soldier, meeting the criteria for a charge sale, refuses to sign the DA Form 3078, the unit commander may certify on the DA Form 3078 in the remarks section that—

(1) The individual received the clothing.

(2) The issuance of the clothing was necessary.

(3) The enlisted Soldier refused to sign the DA Form 3078.

3–11. Processing individual charge sales (payroll deduction)

Unit supply personnel will use DA Form 3078 to make individual charge sales (payroll deductions). A completed DA Form 3078 (see fig 3–1) is required in conjunction with DD Form 139 (Pay Adjustment Authorization) (see fig 3–2) when processing an individual charge sale.

a. Preparation. Supply personnel from the enlisted Soldier's assigned unit will prepare DA Form 3078 in original and three copies. Copy three will be retained in the unit. Place a check in the "Individual Charge Sale" block, and place the following in the remarks block:

(1) The date of separation or discharge.

(2) The date of departure from the installation if scheduled for confinement.

(3) A statement giving the reason for issue.

(4) A statement indicating payment will be deducted from the Soldier's pay.

b. Verification. The enlisted Soldier will present the original and two copies of DA Form 3078 and DD Form 139 to the local finance office or servicing Defense Finance and Accounting Service (DFAS) to verify the Soldier's pay status.

(1) If the Soldier is not assigned to the installation, DA Form 3078 will be presented to the installation finance office servicing the AMCS.

(2) If the Soldier's servicing DFAS is not at the same installation as the DFAS servicing the AMCS and is not a Defense Joint Military Pay System (DJMS) input station, the DFAS will contact the Soldier's servicing finance office to verify the Soldier's pay status. If the Soldier's servicing finance office cannot be determined or contacted, then contact the Defense Finance and Accounting Services (Inquiries Division) by telephone or email to verify the Soldier's pay status.

(3) Verification and the disbursing station symbol number will be entered on DA Form 3078 and DD Form 139 must be authenticated by the local finance office or DFAS authorized representative. This applies whether the Soldier is or is not on the DJMS.

(4) Return all copies of DA Form 3078 and DD Form 139 to Soldier.

c. Processing and purchase. The enlisted Soldier will present the original and two copies of DA Form 3078 and DD Form 139 to the AMCS sales associate for processing at the time of purchase.

(1) The sales associate will check DA Form 3078 and DD Form 139 to ensure the local finance officer or DFAS has verified the Soldier's pay status.

(2) The sales associate will prepare the original and two copies of DA Form 3078 as follows:

(a) Enter the quantities sold in "ISSUED" column.

(b) Show the condition if other than new.

(3) The cashier will verify the signature of the Soldier and sales associate's entries and will compute the total value of the sale. The Soldier will acknowledge receipt of the purchase by signing the original and two copies of DA Form 3078 and DD Form 139 in the space provided. One copy will be given to the Soldier.

(4) The AMCS will retain one copy of the DA Form 3078 and one copy of the DD Form 139.

(5) AMCS will bill for individual charge sales by creating an invoice and forwarding to the CSO. AMCS will identify the invoice as an individual charge sale and enclose a copy of the DA Form 3078 and DD Form 139. Additional examples of a completed DA Form 3078 are available on the CSO Web site at https://www.tacom.army.mil/ilsc/groups/LCS/CP/cso/index.htm. The required quantities of clothing listed on the DA Form 3078 examples are subject to change based on updates made to CTA 50–900. AMCS will bill for individual charge sales by creating an invoice and forwarding to the CSO. AMCS will identify the invoice as an individual charge sale and enclose a copy of the DA Form 3078 and DD Form 139. The CSO has developed a "DA Form 3078 Sample Booklet" to assist unit commanders, supply personnel, AMCS managers and store associates in preparing the form. The samples are based on policy outlined in AR 700-84 and CTA 50-900. This regulation takes precedence over any inconsistencies noted in the CSO sample booklet

PERSONAL CLOTHING REQUEST

For use of this form, see AR 700-84; the proponent agency is DCS, G-4.

DATA REQUIRED BY THE PRIVACY ACT OF 1974

AUTHORITY: 5 U.S.C. Section 301, Departmental Regulations; 10 U.S.C. Section 3013, Secretary of the Army; Army Regulation 700-84, Issue and Sale of Personal Clothing; and E.O. 9397 as amended.

PRINCIPAL PURPOSE: To provide an accountable document for clothing received by enlisted personnel.

ROUTINE USES: None. The DoD Blanket Routine uses that appear at the beginning of the Army's compilation of system of records apply to this system.

DISCLOSURE: Voluntary. However, failure to provide all the request information will prevent from receiving the allocated clothing.

1. DOCUMENT NO.	2. VOUCHER NO.	3. DATE (YYYYMMDD)
N/A	N/A	20140327

4. NAME (Last, First, MI)	8. DODAAC	9. PRIORITY	10. ARMY MILITARY CLOTHING STORE
Doe, John T.	N/A	N/A	Aberdeen Proving Ground, MD

5. SSN (Last Four)	6. GRADE	11. CATEGORY (Check one)	12. TYPE OF TRANSACTION (Check one)
1234	E-1	✓ Active Army / NG / USAR / IMA / IRR / AGR	✓ Initial / Gratuitous / Replacement / Supplemental / Exchange / Individual Charge Sale

7. ORGANIZATION: Bravo Company, 229th FA Bde, APG, MD 21010

13. INVENTORY		14. PHONE NO.	15. POSTED		16. AUTHORIZED BY
DATE (YYYYMMDD)	BY	(410) 436-0987	DATE (YYYYMMDD)	BY	AR 700-84, Chapter 4, Para 1-2
N/A	N/A		N/A	N/A	17. APPROVED BY: DIGITAL SIGNATURE 123456789 — 18. DATE APPROVED: 20140328

19. QTY AUTH	ISS	20. ARTICLES (Common)	21. SIZE	22. UNIT PRICE	23. TOTAL COST	24. QTY AUTH	ISS	25. ARTICLES (Male)	26. SIZE	27. UNIT PRICE	28. TOTAL COST
1	1	Bag, Duffel, Nylon improved	-------	39.18	39.18	1	1	Belt, Trouser, Ctn Web Black, 45"	-------	3.26	3.26
1	1	Belt, Riggers	36	3.82	3.82	1	1	Buckle,Belt,Web,w/Nkl Undplate	-------	4.24	4.24
1	1	Beret, Wool Black Shade 1593	-------	11.57	11.57	1	1	Coat, Mens, All Wtr, Dbl Breasted	44R	99.87	99.87
2	1	Boot, Combat, HW, Tan*	10R	75.63	75.63	1	1	Coat, Men's, AB 450	44R	121.91	121.91
1	1	Boot, Combat, TW, Type II, Tan***	10R	96.75	96.75	7	7	Drawers, Men's Brief	L	2.09	14.63
2	2	Cap,Patrol,Army Combat Uniform	7 1/4	7.45	14.90	1	1	Necktie, Mens Blk, 56-57.5" Long	-------	5.81	5.81
1	1	Cap, Synthetic Micro Fleece	-------	4.91	4.91	1	1	Shirt, Men's Ctn/Poly, SS, AW 521	17x36	18.24	18.24
4	4	Coat, Army Combat Uniform	MR	44.98	179.92	1	1	Shirt, Men's Ctn/Poly, LS, AW 521	17x36	19.99	19.99
1	1	Drawers, Lightweight Gen III**	MR	16.43	16.43	1	1	Shoes, Mens Drs Blk, Poromeric	10R	43.92	43.92
1	1	Drawers, Midweight Gen III**	MR	27.35	27.35	2	2	Trousers,Men's Poly/Wool AB451	34R	45.64	91.28
1	1	Gloves, Light Duty Utility	L	18.11	18.11	2	2	Undershirt, Men's, White, Ctn**	L	2.80	5.60
2	2	Gloves, Insert, Cold	7	2.03	4.06	------	------	--------------------	-------	0.00	0.00
1	1	Gloves, Leather, Black, Unisex	7	18.04	18.04	------	------	--------------------	-------	0.00	0.00
1	1	Jacket, PFU	L	61.75	61.75			**29. ARTICLES (Female)**			
1	1	Pants, PFU	L	31.23	31.23						
2	1	Shirt, L/S, PFU*	L	7.11	7.11	1	------	Belt, Trousers, Ctn Web Blk 1"	-------	0.00	0.00
3	2	Shirt S/S, PFU*	L	5.39	10.78	1	------	Buckle, Belt, Slacks, 1 1/8"	-------	0.00	0.00
7	7	Sock, Boot	10	2.18	15.26	1	------	Coat, All Weather, Dbl Breasted	-------	0.00	0.00
7	7	Sock, Liner, Poly/Nylon, Black	L	1.10	7.70	1	------	Coat,Women's Poly/Wool,AB450	-------	0.00	0.00
4	4	Towel, Bath, Brown**	-------	3.44	13.76	1	------	Neck Tab, Women's Shirt, Blk	-------	0.00	0.00
4	4	Washcloth, Brown**	-------	0.69	2.76	1	------	Shirt, Wm's, Army White, LS 521	-------	0.00	0.00
4	4	Trouser, Army Combat Uniform	MR	44.34	177.36	1	------	Shirt, Wm's, Army White, SS 521	-------	0.00	0.00
3	2	Trunks, PFU*	L	12.07	24.14	1	------	Shoes, Wm's Drs Blk, Poromeric	-------	0.00	0.00
7	7	T-Shirt, Moisture-Wick	L	4.44	31.08	1	------	Skirt, Women's Poly/Wool AB 450	-------	0.00	0.00
1	1	Undershirt, Lightweight Gen III**	L	20.74	20.74	1	------	Slks,Women's Poly/Wool AB 451	-------	0.00	0.00
1	1	Undershirt, Midweight Gen III**	L	37.28	37.28	------	------	--------------------	-------	0.00	0.00
------	------	----------------	-------	0.00	0.00	------	------	--------------------	-------	0.00	0.00
------	------	----------------	-------	0.00	0.00			**TOTAL VALUE**			1,380.37

30. REMARKS
* Must maintain one less than quantity shown
** Issued during initial entry training only
*** May maintain either combat boot
Initial issue for PVT Doe

31. SIGNATURE OF RECIPIENT

DIGITAL SIGNATURE 123456789

DA FORM 3078, MAY 2014 — PREVIOUS EDITIONS ARE OBSOLETE — APD LF v1.00 ES

Figure 3–1. Example of a completed DA Form 3078

PAY ADJUSTMENT AUTHORIZATION			NOTE: If member has been transferred, forward this authorization to the officer currently maintaining the member's pay record.			
MEMBER (Last name) Doe	(First) John	(Middle) T.	SSAN XXX-XX-1234	GRADE/RANK/RATE E-5/SGT	BRANCH OF SERVICE Army	DATE 20140327
PAY GRADE NO. N/A	LAST PAY RECORD EXAMINED If Known		AMOUNT $ 0.00	APPROPRIATION DATA To be entered by AMCS or DFAS "E034541"		

FROM: Service Member Unit Address

NAME OF ACCOUNTABLE D.O.: Name of local Accountable Disbursing Officer (FAO Officer)

SYMBOL NO.: Local Finance **G.A.O. EXCEPTION CODE**: N/A

TO: Local Defense Military Pay Office Mailing Address

YOU ARE HEREBY AUTHORIZED TO [X] CHARGE [ ] CREDIT THE MILITARY PAY RECORD OF THE MEMBER LISTED ABOVE

EXPLANATION AND/OR REASON FOR ADJUSTMENT

- The Unit Commander or Supply representative will place a check in the "Charge" block for Individual Charge Sales, also enter the Soldier's date of separation or discharge.
- A Statement from the Unit Commander or Supply representative is needed to justify reason for issue.
- The Army Military Clothing Store (AMCS) is to ensure that the correct price is annotated on both documents (DA Form 3078 and DA Form 139).
- The total amount will be collected from the Soldier's next available pay.
- All AMCS Managers will use the Army's Appropriation Code: "E034541" on the DD Form 139 in the Appropriation Data Block.
- A signature and date is required by the Soldier to acknowledge receipt of purchase.
- Use continuation sheet as necessary.

____John T. Doe_____   ___20140327_____
Soldier's Signature   Date

List clothing items as indicated on the receipt as follows:
8415-01-586-0103 Coat Army Combat Uniform   2ea $44.98 $89.96
8415-01-519-8277 Trousers Army Combat Uniform 2pr $44.34 $88.68
8430-01-514-4935 Boot Combat Hot Weather   1pr $75.63 $75.63
                                               Total Cost $254.27

Must ensure cost is the same as the prices listed in the AMCS prior to processing thru Finance. Once Finance has completed all blocks under certificate (below) only than could the unit process this form through the Army Military Clothing Store.

Note: Unit must verify that the Soldier has at least 60 days remaining in service prior to the processing of this form. The local finance officer must verify the Soldier's pay status on the DD Form 139 and certify the status for debt collection to begin.

The above adjustment is based on a thorough examination of all available records. If the Disbursing Officer has knowledge that a previous adjustment has been made or why the adjustment should not be made for the same item, this authorization should be returned with a brief statement of the reason for failure to make adjustment.

FROM: B Co, 1st Bn, Fort Campbell, KY 12345-0001

CERTIFYING OFFICER (Name, rank/grade, and signature): Jane B. Doe, CPT

CERTIFICATE: I CERTIFY that the adjustment indicated above has been entered on the above-named member's Military Pay Record. (If adjustment has not been entered, give explanation on reverse over D.O.'s signature and symbol number.)

TO: Sender's Mailing Address

TYPED NAME AND GRADE OF D.O.: Local Disbursing Officer
D.O. SYMBOL NO.: Local Finance **DATE**: 20140331
SIGNATURE: DIGITAL SIGNATURE 123456789

DD FORM 139, MAY 53 — EDITION OF THIS FORM NOT HAVING SSAN IS OBSOLETE AFTER 30 JUN 69.   Form approved by Comp. Gen., U.S. April 23, 1953

Adobe Designer 8.0

Figure 3–2. Example of a completed DD Form 139

3–12. Internet sales or sales through the Exchange call center

a. Introduction.

(1) Persons authorized to buy from AMCS may order from the Army Military Clothing Store Sales Web site at http://www.aafes.com, or orders may be placed by calling the telephone numbers listed below:

(a) Order by phone: 1–800–527–2345.

(b) Order by FAX: 1–800–446–0163.

(c) TDD 1–800–423–2011.

(d) Commercial: 1–214–465–6690.

(2) Customers located outside the United States may call the commercial number, which will not permit collect calls, or utilize the following international numbers.

(a) Belgium 0800–7–2432.

(b) Germany 0800–82–16500.

(c) Guam 01800–636–3297.

(d) Italy 8008–71227.

(e) Japan or Okinawa 00531–11–4132.

(f) Korea 00308–13–0664.

(g) Netherlands 0800–022–1889.

(h) Spain 900–971–391.

(i) Turkey 00800–18–488–6312 (Use off-base commercial lines as calls cannot be made from phones on base).

(j) United Kingdom 0800–96–8101.

(3) Address technical questions or requests for special measurement uniforms to Fort Sam Houston AMCS toll-free; individual catalogs may be obtained by using these numbers:

(a) Phone: 800–527–2345 (Commercial 1–210–221–3794, 1–210–221–4656, 1–210–221–5111, or 1–210–221–3797).

(b) FAX: 800–446–0163.

(c) Defense switched network (DSN) 471–3794.

b. Exchanges. Exchanges (except for size or material defects and refunds) other than for overpayment are prohibited. Items returned for exchange must be shipped in the same condition as when received.

c. Transportation charges. For all mail-order shipments, transportation charges will be prepaid. Items are normally shipped within 2 working days. Additional fees apply to upgrade the normal shipping priorities.

3–13. Sale of defective, soiled, or damaged Defense Logistics Agency-Troop Support merchandise

a. If the AMCS receives defective merchandise, they are required to coordinate with the CSO to process a SF 368. Process an SF 364 (Report of Discrepancy (ROD)) or DD Form 361 (Transportation Discrepancy Report (TDR)) when merchandise is received in a soiled or damaged condition. In these instances, the items will be retained until disposition instructions are received from DLA–TS.

b. If an item was damaged or soiled after receipt, or if the AMCS is directed to dispose of an item that was reported on a SF 368, the AMCS manager will determine if the item can be economically repaired or cleaned and restored to at least Condition Code B, 75 percent wear condition. Condition Code B garments will be marked "Condition Code B, 75 percent wear" in an area that will not render the garment unserviceable.

c. The item will be returned to stock as either Condition Code A or Condition Code B if it can be economically repaired or cleaned (at a cost of no more than 25 percent of standard price). Costs incurred in restoring the item to salable condition will be paid for using operating costs.

d. If item cannot be restored to Condition Code B condition, the sale price will be reduced until it sells or until, in the judgment of the manager, there is no market for it.

e. The item will be turned in to the DRMS under locally established procedures if it cannot be sold.

3–14. Reporting shipping and packaging discrepancies

AMCS will notify the CSO of any shipping or packaging discrepancy and request submission of a SF 364 in accordance with Exchange Operating Procedure (EOP) 40–4. EOP 40–4 is accessible through the CSO Army knowledge online Web site at https://www.us.army.mil/suite/page/633544.

3–15. Price reductions

a. Price reductions (when approved by the DCS, G–4), to stimulate sales of phase-out items in the AMCS, are authorized only when there is a difference in utility or desirability of an item because of age, condition or model. The purpose of such reductions in price is to recognize the relative value in use of the item concerned and to encourage supply economy through usage of such material. To be justified, price reductions will serve to reduce procurement requirements for a standard item or items.

(1) Price reductions will be offered as early as possible in the development process of new items.

(2) Coordination of phase-out or phase-in plans must be ongoing between HQDA, DLA, AMC, U.S. Army Soldier and Biological Chemical Command, Program Executive Office, Soldier, Integrated Materiel Management Center, the Exchange, CSO, DLA–TS, and TRADOC.

 (a) The CSO will consider the worldwide AMCS and CIIP assets of phase-out items in developing the supply request package, which includes phase-out, or phase-in plans for new item introduction.

 1. The phase-in or phase-out plans will include utilization of AMCS worldwide assets.

 2. The estimated date of supply will be established to allow optimum use of AMCS stocks along with other assets of phase-out items.

 3. Plans will include maximum utilization of AMCS assets of phase-out items by the CIIP where economically feasible.

 (b) CSO will coordinate with TRADOC and AMCS to ensure assets are transferred to CIIP at current AMCS prices. No operating costs will be charged for AMCS items transferred to CIIP.

 (c) CSO will inform DLA–TS of quantities transferred from AMCS assets to fill CIIP requirements.

 (d) At least 18 months prior to the estimated date of supply of new items, the decision to implement price reduction will be made based on the following criteria:

 1. After maximum use of AMCS stocks to fill CIIP requirements, a 25 percent price reduction will be offered, if the AMCS worldwide assets are projected to be 3 months or fewer of stock on hand.

 2. If, after maximum use of the AMCS stocks to fill CIIP requirements, Exchange worldwide assets are projected to be 3 or more months based on past sales of the item, a 50 percent price reduction will be offered.

 3. Effective date of price reduction implementation will be 12 months prior to the estimated date of supply of the new item.

 (e) After price reductions are initiated, the Exchange headquarters will ensure that AMCS does not requisition additional phase-out items.

 (f) After initial price reduction, decision will be made on length of time reduced prices will be in effect based on quantities of stock remaining.

 1. Based on quantity of AMCS stock on hand, a reduction of 25 or 50 percent of original price will be made (12th month through 6th month before the estimated date of supply).

 2. A reduction of 75 percent of original sales price, if necessary, will be made 6th month through the estimated date of supply or until stocks reach optimum economic point.

 3. The CSO or Exchange will advise DLA–TS of results and changes in assets after review.

 4. Other reductions may be implemented after quarterly inventory review.

 (g) Condition Code B, 75 percent wear items will be sold at 50 percent of the price of Condition Code A items.

 b. During the phase-out or phase-in of clothing items in the AMCS, the DCS, G–4 will provide funding to support inventory requirements for phase-in items. The Exchange proceeds from the phase-out items will be used as an offset to fund the new requirement.

 c. The price reduction will be offset by a decrease to the "inventory with agent" account so that the Exchange accountability to the Army is reduced by the amount of the price reduction. This will be accommodated during the year-end reconciliation of inventories. The Army "loss" will be confined to price reduction for those quantities currently on hand with the Exchange.

3–16. Transfer of Condition Code B clothing
Clothing generated by the local installation supply division or forward distribution point and classified as Condition Code B may be transferred to the AMCS, with reimbursement to the generating activity. A memorandum or other suitable document can be used to offer these items to the AMCS. As a minimum, the document will contain the national stock number, nomenclature, size, unit of issue, price and quantity. The AMCS may, at their option, accept items offered; local procedures will be developed for transfer of these items.

Chapter 4
Allowances Under the Clothing Monetary Allowance System

4–1. Initial allowances of personal clothing
 a. CTA 50–900 lists initial and supplemental clothing allowances authorized for enlisted Soldiers. The initial allowance permitted for those enlisted Soldiers listed in paragraph 4–2 will not be considered as the "last authorization to an initial allowance" when determining entitlement to a CMA.

b. DA Form 3078, when submitted to AMCS, will contain a statement explaining reasons for the initial issue. Orders will be attached to the DA Form 3078. This statement will identify the appropriate category of personnel shown in paragraph 4–2a through 4–2h. For ARNG or USAR personnel entering the Active Army, they will contact their supply personnel to order clothing through the Kentucky Logistics Operation Center.

4–2. Personnel entitled to initial allowances
Initial clothing allowances are authorized for the following:

a. An individual on first enlistment or induction.

b. An individual who reenlists after 90 days from the date of last discharge. The discharge date will be placed in the remarks block of the clothing request.

c. A prisoner restored to duty after sentence to confinement or punitive discharge imposed by a court martial.

d. Enlisted Soldiers of an inactive reserve unit who do not attend weekend or annual training or who are not authorized clothing allowances in accordance with CTA 50–900 are authorized a complete initial issue allowance. The enlisted Soldier must have been separated 90 days or more from the Active Army. Enlisted Soldiers with fewer than 90 days of separation time from the Active Army will have all clothing items in their possession when discharged. The date of separation must be indicated in the remarks block of the clothing request. In addition, substandard items in their possession may be replaced if they do not meet Army standards of appearance.

e. An enlisted Soldier who did not receive the complete initial allowance or was required to turn-in clothing at time of discharge or release from active duty. The initial allowance authorized these Soldiers will be reduced by the amount of clothing they retained on discharge or release from active duty. A copy of the discharge certificate and a copy of reenlistment orders will accompany the issue request.

f. Retired enlisted Soldiers recalled to active duty after 90 days from date of last release from active duty or date of retirement. Only one such entitlement will accrue during any 4 consecutive years.

g. A Soldier enlisting from another Service without regard to date of discharge from the previous Service.

h. Officers or warrant officers separated from the Service who enlist or reenlist for other than retirement reasons. Only one entitlement will accrue during any 4 consecutive years.

4–3. Clothing monetary allowance or clothing replacement allowance

a. Monetary allowances. In all areas where CMA is in effect, personal clothing initially provided at Government expense will be maintained up to the prescribed allowances by enlisted Soldiers at their own expense. A clothing replacement allowance for the cost of replacement and purchase of new items will be paid to the enlisted Soldiers annually on the anniversary month the Soldier entered the service. This allowance will be paid along with, and in addition to, regular pay. The CRA also may be used to buy additional quantities of personal clothing items. The intent of the CRA is not to cover the normal costs of cleaning, laundering, and pressing personal clothing. There are two types of CRA, basic and standard. The monetary values of these allowances are published annually.

(1) *Basic clothing replacement allowance.* Each enlisted Soldier will be entitled to receive the basic CRA. The allowance begins to accumulate on the day after the Soldier completes 6 months (180 days) of active duty service. If the Soldier enters a non-duty or non-pay status at any time during this period, time lost is not regarded. This is not authority for payment of the allowance when in a non-pay and allowance status. The 6-month (180 days) period begins on the date of last authorization to the initial clothing allowance. The basic CRA will be paid for the remainder of the first 3 years of continuous active duty. The basic CRA is 70 percent of the standard CRA.

(2) *Standard monetary allowance.* Each enlisted Soldier will be entitled to the standard clothing replacement allowance beginning the day after the Soldier completes 36 months of active duty. If the Soldier enters a non-duty or non-pay status at any time during this period, time lost is not regarded. This is not authority for payment of the allowance when in a non-pay and allowance status. On the 37th month, the standard CRA will begin. An enlisted Soldier who reenlists within 3 months after the date previous enlistment terminates is not considered to have a break in service for the purpose of this entitlement. The standard CRA will be paid for the remainder of a Soldier's continuous active duty. The standard CRA is the total of allowances paid.

b. Determining entitlement to monetary allowances.

(1) An enlisted Soldier is not entitled to the basic or standard clothing replacement allowance if in a temporary commissioned or warrant officer status. This time cannot be counted in determining eligibility for basic or standard monetary allowances.

(2) Enlisted Soldiers ordered to active duty from reserve status are entitled to a basic CRA after completion of 6 months (180 days) of active duty service.

(3) A monetary allowance will not be paid in a command where the CMA system is not in effect. Allowances will be discontinued as prescribed in paragraph 4–3c. Time served in such a command will be counted in determining eligibility for the basic or standard CRA when a Soldier returns to an area where the monetary allowance is paid. Any ARNG personnel ordered to active duty in excess of 179 days are entitled to the CRA after 6 months (180 days) active duty even though assigned to the ARNG.

(4) Prisoners in a nonpay and allowance status, including those in restoration training, will not be paid a CRA.

Rather, these persons will be supplied necessary clothing items at Government expense on an issue-in-kind basis. See chapter 5 for other information on clothing for prisoners.

(5) Prisoners in a pay and allowance status will continue to be paid the CRA. Prisoners will replace, at their own expense, personal clothing that the installation correctional officer decides is needed to perform their duties while in confinement. Soldiers confined at other than their home station must also pay for clothing items required for travel to home station.

(6) Soldiers enlisting in the Active Army from the RCs within 90 days of release from active duty are entitled to receive the basic clothing replacement allowance. This allowance commences on the day after the Soldier completes 6 months (180 days) of continuous active duty service.

c. Discontinuance of clothing monetary allowance. Action will be taken by the custodian of the Soldier's pay record in the issue-in-kind area to discontinue the clothing monetary allowances. The pay order commencing foreign duty pay may be used for this purpose. The effective date of discontinuance will be at 2400 hours on the day before departure from the clothing monetary allowance area.

d. Reinstatement under the clothing monetary allowance. The custodian of a Soldier's pay record reinstates payment of the clothing replacement allowance. Resumption of the allowance will be at 0001 hours on the day of departure from the issue-in-kind area.

4–4. Increase in authorized allowances
An increase in an allowance will not be retroactive except when a Soldier that is in service before the effective date of the increase is authorized a supplemental allowance and must purchase additional items by some future specified date.

4–5. Replacement of initial allowances with new items
When new items, other than insignia, are adopted to replace initial allowances, enlisted Soldiers on active duty tours before the effective date of the change must purchase the prescribed quantities of the new items within announced time periods. New items will be introduced with an optional phase-in period. This gives enlisted Soldiers time to save the cost of the new item from their clothing replacement allowance. A fair wear out period is announced when initial clothing allowance items are superseded.

4–6. Supplemental clothing allowance
In addition to the initial allowance for personal clothing for enlisted Soldiers, the authorized supplemental allowances in CTA 50–900, will be provided as a supplemental issue. Only one issue may be approved during any period of continuous service in the type of duty for which the supplemental allowance is authorized.

a. Unit supply personnel will fill out the DA Form 3078 in accordance with paragraph 1–6p and place the following statement in the remarks block: "Individual has not received a full or partial supplemental issue while assigned to duties authorized a supplemental allowance in CTA 50–900." Unit supply personnel will attach proper documentation of MOS to the DA Form 3078 for all supplemental issues. If a supplemental issue was provided and there was a break of 3 years or more between MOS assignments requiring a supplemental issue, unit supply personnel will place the date the supplemental issue was made in the remarks block. Once the supplemental issue is made, the DA Form 3078 transfers with the Soldier. Normal replacements thereafter will be at the expense of the Soldier.

b. Soldiers are required to maintain supplemental issues for 3 years or completion of the duty for which the items were provided, whichever is greater.

4–7. Supplemental allowance authorization
CTA 50-900 contains authorized supplemental allowances. Commands may request to modify or establish supplemental allowances by submitting DA Form 5965 (Basis of Issue for Clothing and Individual Equipment (CIE)), through command channels, using the guidance provided in CTA 50–900, to the DCS, G–4 (DALO–SUI), 500 Army Pentagon, Washington, DC 20310–0500. The DCS, G–4 is the approval authority for supplemental allowances. The Chief, Army Reserve and the CNGB may reduce the supplemental allowance as needs dictate.

4–8. Army Service uniform payment and accounting
a. Recruiters and Medal of Honor recipients are authorized a cash allowance to purchase ASU components. The allowance will not exceed—

(1) The current Exchange price, when the authorized items are available from military sources. AMCSs are considered military sources.

(2) The current Exchange price, in cases where at least one uniform (coat, trousers, skirts, and necessary accessories) must be purchased from commercial or nonmilitary sources.

b. The cash allowance will be applied to the purchase of an ASU consisting of a cap, coat, and low-waist trousers for male Soldiers, or a hat, coat, skirt, and slacks for female Soldiers, and the necessary accessories. The ASU will be purchased within 30 days of receipt of the cash allowance. When necessary, the commander will grant an additional 30-day extension.

c. An additional authorized allowance can be applied to the ASU for alterations. The amount must be documented on an alteration slip and can be obtained for the following accoutrements:

(1) Shoulder epaulets.

(2) Rank chevrons.

(3) Service stripes.

Note. The Army will pay for these alterations, not to exceed the current Exchange price for the total cost of the alterations.

d. On assignment as Sergeant Major of the Army, a supplemental clothing allowance is authorized for purchase of additional uniforms (see CTA 50–900).

e. The unit commander will authorize preparation of SF 1034 (Public Voucher for Purchases and Services Other Than Personal) in the proper amount with a statement on the voucher as follows: "The supplemental allowance is authorized by CTA 50–900."

f. Collection action will be brought against the Soldier if the prescribed items of clothing are not purchased within 30 days from the date of receipt of this allowance or approved extension (see para 4–8b).

g. The unit commander will sign the proper block before sending the SF 1034 to the finance and accounting office, or the U.S. Property and Fiscal Office (USPFO) for ARNG, for payment. Forward the SF 1034 in original and three copies with two copies of the order assigning the Soldier to recruiting duty or awarding the Soldier the Medal of Honor to the servicing DFAS for payment. The DFAS will forward a paid copy to the unit (or USPFO for ARNG), for filing. Funds to be charged for payment of this allowance are MPA (P 1118), National Guard personnel, Army (P–), and reserve personnel, Army (RPA).

4–9. Maternity uniform

a. Female enlisted Soldiers are authorized to wear the maternity ASU (maternity shirt, skirt, slacks and tunic listed in CTA 50–900) when the Soldier's condition becomes obvious in a regularly fitted uniform. The enlisted Soldier will maintain ASU maternity uniforms items for 3 years. If 3 years have lapsed since an authorization for a supplemental issue of maternity uniform items has occurred, a new authorization may be approved. The ASU maternity uniform items are a supplemental issue and are not in the supply system; therefore, Soldiers will procure them from an AMCS.

b. Upon receipt of certification by a doctor that the enlisted Soldier is pregnant, the unit supply sergeant or specialist will—

(1) Verify the current uniform price with the AMCS.

(2) Fill out the DA Form 3078 in accordance with paragraph 1–6p, for supplemental issue, with the following statement in block 30 (remarks): "Issued as supplemental items as authorized by CTA 50–900" (see para 4–6).

(3) Enclose a copy of the doctor's certification (physical profile).

c. Print an original and four copies of the DA Form 3078. One copy will be retained in the unit suspense file and one copy will be transferred with the Soldier.

d. The maternity ACU is an OCIE item and will be requested in accordance with the procedures contained in DA Pam 710–2–1 from the local CIF. While the maternity ACU remains principally an organizational issue item, Soldiers may special order additional quantities, if desired, from the AMCS. The unit commander will determine if the Soldier will be issued all or a partial maternity allowance, depending on the Soldier's duty assignment.

4–10. Clothing and footwear for Soldiers allergic to fabric, dye, or metal

Soldiers allergic to fabric, dye, or metal may obtain protective clothing as follows:

a. Obtain a doctor's certificate certifying the allergy and present it to the AMCS or the CIIP, as appropriate.

b. Forward a DD Form 1348 (DOD Single Line Item Requisition System Document (Manual)) or a DD Form 150 (Special Measurements Blank for Special Measurements/Orthopedic Boots and Shoes) with a doctor's certificate for footwear to the DLA–TS, 700 Robins Avenue (Building 3A Station 4121), Philadelphia, PA 19111–5098. Ensure the form used contains the Soldier's name, rank, social security number, size, and type of footwear for each foot with a problem.

c. Replacement of clothing items requires a doctor's certificate containing the reason or circumstances for the replacement. Local procedures may be adopted.

Chapter 5
Personal Clothing Issue Procedures

5–1. Obtaining personal clothing items

a. Obtaining personal clothing items DA Form 3078 will be the only document used to obtain personal clothing items for Active Army enlisted Soldiers, Individual Ready Reserve (IRR), individual mobilization augmentation (IMA), USAR enlisted Soldiers attending IET, and ARNG enlisted Soldiers attending IET. The DA Form 3078 is an auditable document. The form is subject to formal and informal auditing and is a receipt for the enlisted Soldier. Only original signatures or when using the automated DA Form, a digital signature will be accepted; stamps or photocopies of signatures are not acceptable. A digital signature will be required on the automated DA Form 3078. It is also a supporting document for the unit and FAO. The ARNG and USAR TPU requestors supported by the Central Clothing Distribution Facility (CCDF) will use the electronic or printed forms prescribed in the CCD User Handbook (CCDF Form 2 (Request for Access Form), CCDF Form 3 (Personal Clothing Request), CCDF Form 3078 (CCDF Mail or FAX Request) New Garments), CCDF Form 3078–1 (Personal Clothing Request), CCDF Form 3078-2 (CCDF Mail or FAX Request) Recycled Garments)."

a. The DA Form 3078, processed at the AMCS for an ARNG Soldier on initial active duty for training (IADT) must be accompanied by two copies of the Soldier's orders. The accounting classification to be charged will be annotated on the orders and entered in block 30 of the DA Form 3078. The AMCS will retain one copy of the orders and forward the second copy with the DA Form 3078 to the supporting DFAS.

b. The CIIP or AMCS will not accept an improperly prepared DA Form 3078; forms dated over 30 days prior to the processing date will not be accepted.

c. Seasonal or deferred issues of specified CB items at CIIPs will be accomplished as directed by the ACOMs.

5–2. Issue of items to enlisted Soldiers during initial processing

a. Preparing DA Form 3078. The CIIPs normally prepare the DA Form 3078 using Automated Clothing Initial Issue Point System procedures. To prepare a manual DA Form 3078, use ink or indelible pencil. In the "approved by block" enter the name, rank, branch and signature of the unit commander or their commissioned or warrant officer representative (exceptions to policy will be on an individual basis approved by DALO–SUI). The signature must agree with DA Form 1687 maintained at the CIIP or DA Form 7000 for AMCS. When providing the DA Form 7000 to the AMCS, the gaining unit must also attach an original or copy of the organization assumption of command orders signed by the commander. See figure 5–1 for an example of a completed DA Form 7000. Only original signatures will be accepted on the manual DA Form 3078, ink type stamps or photocopies of signatures are not acceptable. Prepare an original and four copies when forwarding a manual DA Form 3078 to an AMCS or CIIP. The unit will retain one copy and forward the original and three copies to the AMCS or CIIP.

DELEGATION OF AUTHORITY - ARMY MILITARY CLOTHING STORES					1. EXPIRATION DATE (YYYYMMDD)
For use of this form, see AR 700-84; the proponent agency is DCS, G-4.					20150327
2. UNIT/ACTIVITY Bravo Company, 229th FA Bde			3. LOCATION Aberdeen Proving Ground, MD 21010		

Commissioned officer or warrant officer individual(s) listed below are authorized to approve DA Form 3078 *(Block 17)* submitted to Army Military Clothing Stores

4. LAST NAME	FIRST NAME	MIDDLE INITIAL *(Typed)*	5. RANK	6. SIGNATURE
Doe, Jane T.			2LT	
Doe, John B.			1LT	
----------Nothing Follows----------			----------	
N/A			----------	

Individuals listed below are authorized to sign "Signature of Recipient" block *(Block 31)* of DA Form 3078

7. LAST NAME	FIRST NAME	MIDDLE INITIAL *(Typed)*	8. RANK	9. SIGNATURE
Doe, Mary M.			SPC	
Doe, James T.			SSG	
----------Nothing Follows----------			----------	
N/A			----------	

10. DODAAC	11. UNIT/ACTIVITY TELEPHONE NUMBER	12. DATE (YYYYMMDD)
W54ABC	DSN - 584-1234 COMMERCIAL (410) 436-1234	20140326

13. LAST NAME	FIRST NAME	MIDDLE INITIAL *(Typed)*	14. RANK	15. SIGNATURE
Doe, Jimmy D.			CPT	**DIGITAL SIGNATURE 123456789**

DA FORM 7000, MAY 2014   EDITION OF MAY 93 IS OBSOLETE.   APD LF v1.00ES

Figure 5–1. Example of a completed DA Form 7000

b. Preparation and instructions for DA Form 3078. Preparation and instructions for DA Form 3078 are contained in figure 3–1.

(1) Responsible unit/activity personnel will complete DA Form 3078 in original and four copies. Leave blocks 1, 2, 9, 13, and 15 blank. Mark block 12 (TYPE OF TRANSACTION), Initial. In block 16, enter AR 700–84, as appropriate. The funding appropriation will be entered in block 30 by the resource manager.

(2) The unit commander or activity supervisor will indicate in blocks 19 and 24, REQ column, the quantity of items authorized for issue. The approving authority will enter their name and sign in block 17. Enter date signed in block 18. Commanders will ensure the DA Form 3078 is properly completed before signing the form.

(3) Individual will receive from the AMCS those authorized clothing items as indicated on DA Form 3078. AMCS will complete applicable blocks. Unit is responsible for ensuring cost information is placed in block 30. Upon completion of transaction, individual will sign block 31 of the original and all copies.

c. Distribution of DA Form 3078.

(1) The unit retains one copy as an accountable document for future reference.

(2) On completion of the issue, the CIIP or AMCS forwards the original and one copy to servicing finance office for payment.

(3) The individual retains one copy.

(4) The unit retains one completed copy until the Soldier has completed 6 months (180 days) of service and has received all of the initial issue items.

(a) Upon transfer or permanent change of station during the first 6 months (180 days) of active duty, a copy remains with the Soldier's record and is taken to the new assigned unit.

(b) After 6 months (180 days) of active duty are completed, an inventory and inspection of the enlisted Soldier's clothing and footwear will be accomplished. If all required clothing and footwear are on hand and in a serviceable

condition, the unit's copy of the DA Form 3078 will be destroyed. Upon destruction of the DA Form 3078, each enlisted Soldier retains personal responsibility for the initial issue of clothing and is subject to charges of financial liability in the event any of the clothing items become lost, damaged, or destroyed. Enlisted Soldiers have personal responsibility for clothing issued to them under a supplemental issue and are subject to charges of financial liability in the event of loss, damage or destruction. DA Form 3078 will be retained for RC Soldiers per paragraph 12–5.

d. Special measurement clothing. The need for special measurement clothing and footwear as discussed in chapter 7 is determined during initial processing. Full allowances will be expeditiously obtained. All copies of DA Form 3078 will be stamped or marked "special measurement" at the time of processing.

e. Alteration service. Complete alterations to garments will be completed no later than 4 days after initial processing.

f. Undergarments. Female undergarments are a one-time cash purchase as part of the initial clothing allowance for females. Unit commanders must afford female Soldiers the opportunity to purchase these items.

5–3. Issue of personal clothing items during other than initial processing

a. Issue of clothing, at times other than initial processing, includes any of the following authorized transactions if DA Form 3078 is used:

(1) Completion of initial allowances.

(2) Completion of supplemental allowances.

(3) Gratuitous issues.

(4) Individual charge sales (payroll deduction).

(5) Exchanges.

(6) Temporary issues from the unit's or correctional facility's excess supply.

b. Instructions for filling out the DA Form 3078 are outlined in paragraph 1–6*p*.

c. An original and three copies of DA Form 3078 must be prepared. The original and two copies will be sent to the AMCS; the third copy will be held in suspense at the unit. Exceptions are as follows:

(1) *Completion of initial allowances.* Enlisted Soldiers must show proof of turn in or non-receipt. Their original DA Form 3078 with zeroed entries must be attached to the new request—

(a) For requests from new enlistees.

(b) For Soldiers reenlisting, requests for replacement of items turned in.

(c) When initial issue allowances were not completed.

(2) *Supplemental allowances.* For guidance on supplemental allowances, see paragraph 4–6.

(3) *Gratuitous issues.* For guidance on gratuitous issues, see paragraph 5–4.

(4) *Individual charge sales (payroll deduction).* For guidance on individual charge sales, see paragraph 3–10.

(5) *Exchanges.* For guidance on exchanges, see paragraphs 5–11 and 5–12.

(6) *Temporary issues.* For guidance on temporary issues, see paragraph 5–8*a*.

5–4. Gratuitous issue

Claims procedures in accordance with AR 27–20 apply to both officer and enlisted personnel for the replacement of clothing bag items lost, damaged, or destroyed while a Soldier is in the Service. Costs for the gratuitous issue will be processed using the Military Personnel Army funds. An example of claims procedures would be baggage lost during travel by military conveyance. Gratuitous issues will be received from the CIIP when located on a CIIP installation for designated personnel (such as, drill and platoon sergeants) and at the AMCS.

a. Authority for issuing ASUs and component items for burial of a deceased active duty Soldier (officer or enlisted) is in accordance with DA Pam 638–2. The appropriate base operation accounting classification will be placed in the "REMARKS" block of the DA Form 3078.

b. Unit supply sergeants and specialists will use the DA Form 3078 for gratuitous issue. Instructions for filling out the DA Form 3078 are outlined in paragraph 1–6*p*.

c. DA Form 3078 will contain a statement indicating specific reason for the gratuitous issue in block 30.

d. Clothing may be replaced when authorized by Army medical departments.

(1) To prevent spread of contagious diseases, clothing will be destroyed under these circumstances. Clothing items may be replaced by gratuitous issue for both enlisted and officer personnel.

(2) An enlisted Soldier with a deformity or inability to wear certain items may exchange items of personal clothing, such as woolen clothing and combat boots, for cotton items or low quarter shoes, provided—

(a) The physical condition was not in whole or in part the fault or neglect of the enlisted Soldier while in active Federal service.

(b) The medical department considers the enlisted Soldier fit for continued military service.

(3) A gratuitous issue for an enlisted Soldier and officers are authorized to replace items damaged when administering emergency first aid to another Servicemember.

(4) A gratuitous issue for officer and enlisted personnel are authorized to replace items of clothing caused by

excessive weight loss or gain after an officer or enlisted Soldier has had surgery. A medical statement stating reason for the weight loss or gain will be submitted along with the DA Form 3078.

(5) Officer or enlisted personnel clothing may be replaced because of contamination. When submitting DA Form 3078 to AMCS, attach a statement of contamination provided by proper authorities along with a statement provided by unit commander. Contamination may be medically or organically related. Contaminated clothing must be destroyed by appropriate personnel.

e. Clothing is replaced at no cost to the officer or enlisted Soldier if the clothing is lost or damaged by an in-house operated Government laundry, or dry cleaning facility. The laundry facility manager will prepare and approve the DA Form 3078. The appropriate base operations accounting classification will be placed in the remarks block, charging the laundry and dry cleaning account. For contracted facilities, follow instructions contained in AR 210 130.

f. The officer or enlisted Soldier pays for replacing items of personal clothing lost, damaged, or destroyed while in a commercial business establishment.

g. The officer or enlisted Soldier must use claims procedures for clothing lost, damaged, or destroyed in field laundry units during exercises.

h. If unusual circumstances exist that neither meet the criteria specified in paragraphs 5-4a through e, nor qualify for claims procedures, a request for exception to policy may be submitted to the first general officer in the Soldier's chain of command for approval. Each DA Form 3078 submitted for approval will be evaluated prior to approval. If approval is granted, a copy of the approved correspondence will be attached to the DA Form 3078 so that the AMCS or CIIP manager will honor the request. A form letter/blanket approval is not acceptable. Approval may only be for quantities of clothing bag items authorized in CTA 50-900.

i. Officers and enlisted Soldiers that are evacuated from the theater of operations to a medical treatment facility (MTF) because of injuries or illness when their personal clothing does not accompany them are authorized a gratuitous issue of specified CB items.

(1) The Commander of the MTF will authorize the issue, on a gratuitous basis, of uniform items sufficient to meet the Soldiers' needs. Also, this guidance applies to Soldiers being treated on an in/out-patient basis, who are assigned to the warrior transition unit (WTU) and are in a medical hold status. The installation commander will authorize the gratuitous issue in these cases.

(2) Gratuitous issue of specified clothing bag items are authorized for officer and enlisted Soldiers based on individual requirements. The following items are authorized:

Table 5–1
Gratuitous issue of specified clothing bag items

Personal clothing items	QTY authorized
ACU coat and trousers	2 each
Boot, combat, tan	1 pair
Drawers, sand (male)	4 each
Patrol cap	1 each
T-shirt, moisture wicking sand	4 each
Duffel bag	1 each
Belt rigger, sand	1 each
Socks, boot, green	4 pair
IPFU jacket	1 each
IPFU pants	1 each
IPFU trunks	2 each
IPFU long sleeve shirt	1 each
IPFU short sleeve shirt	2 each
Gloves insert, cold foliage green	1 pair
Gloves, flexor, light duty	1 pair

(3) The AMCS will issue selected CB items and the CIF will be utilized for the issuance of selected OCIE items (both gratuitous) to Wounded Warriors.

j. The gratuitous issue will not include Army Service Uniform items or items that do not normally deploy with Soldiers. Exception to this provision provides that an officer or enlisted member awarded the Medal of Honor (active duty or retired) are entitled to the following CB and optional items:

Table 5–2
Medal of honor recipient authorization

Personal clothing items	QTY authorized
ASU coat	2 each
ASU trousers	2 pair
Long sleeve white shirts	2 each
Short sleeve white shirts	2 each
Black belt	1 each
Buckle	1 each
Black tie (four hand)	1 each
Bow tie	1 pair
Beret (black)	1 each
ASU cap (saucer, hat band, cap device, cap strap	1 each
Poromeric shoes (black)	1 each
Socks, liner, polyester/wool black	4 each

(1) Process in obtaining clothing for Medal of Honor recipients is as follows:

(a) Once congressional approval is provided, the DCS, G–4 (DALO–SUI) will notify CSO and Exchange by name and last four of the Soldier's social security number, unit of assignment and Deputy Chief of Staff, G–1 (DCS, G–1) point of contact information.

(b) DCS, G–4 is responsible for the authorization of clothing and the direct coordination with the CSO ensuring the availability of authorized CB items listed in paragraphs 5–1 through 5–4.

(c) DCS, G–1 is responsible for awards and decorations as authorized in accordance with AR 670–1 (OMA funds).

(d) The CSO will initiate a DA Form 3078 upon notification from the DCS, G–4. The approving authority for block 17 of the DA Form 3078 will be signed by the Chief, CSO authorizing the Medal of Honor recipient the authority to pick up clothing at the AMCS. In addition, the CSO will coordinate with Exchange and the AMCS to ensure the availability of clothing as authorized on the DA Form 3078.

(e) The personal clothing request will be expedited by the Army Military Clothing Store upon notification by the CSO or HQ Exchange.

(2) DA Form 3078 (used for gratuitous issue), block 30, remarks must identify the operation (for example, Operation ENDURING FREEDOM, Operation IRAQI FREEDOM) to which the Soldier was deployed or Medal of Honor recipient as awarded by Congressional approval.

(3) Physical fitness socks and female undergarments are commercial items. All Services can procure commercial items in according with 10 USC 1047.

(4) Name tape, U.S. Army patch, unit insignia and rank will be provided to officer and enlisted member using OMA funds or as approved by the authorizing official.

k. Army direct ordering (ADO) is a Web-based program established to provide sustainment of selected OCIE and clothing bag items to Soldiers in support of combat operations. The purpose of ADO is to provide the ASCC commander a capability to sustain individual Soldier's selected OCIE (OMA funds) and clothing bag items (MPA funds) during combat operations.

(1) Soldiers required to deploy into the area of operation with their entire specified OCIE and CB items as prescribed in the DCS, G–1 Personnel Policy Guidance (PPG) and required to sustain these items up to the specified basis of issue (BOI) through ADO. ADO is not for initial issue or to fill shortages. ADO is limited to sustainment of specified OCIE and CB items that are lost, stolen, damaged or destroyed. ADO will not be used to obtain unauthorized OCIE and CB items or items excess to the individual Soldier BOI.

(2) Requests for exceptions to order CB items beyond the individual Soldier BOI quantity will be submitted by the respective commander to the ASCC G–4 for review and sent for DCS, G–4 (DALO–SUI) approval.

(3) In cases of OCIE where the unserviceable item has been lost, stolen, damaged, or destroyed to the point where a direct exchange is not possible or feasible, commanders will follow the appropriate accountability procedures outlined in AR 735–5 to properly account for the item, and then provide the Soldier with a replacement.

(4) Department of Defense Civilians and contractors are not authorized to enroll in the ADO program or order items from the ADO program menu.

(5) Requests for access to ADO will be processed through the ASCC G–4 and sent to the DCS, G–4 (DALO–SUI) for consideration.

5–5. Issue and attachment of insignia

a. Enlisted Soldiers are authorized an initial issue of standard color and subdued insignia if wearing insignia is required because of the following:

(1) Grade.

(2) Years of active service.

(3) Months OCONUS in designated areas.

(4) Assignments.

b. Enlisted Soldiers are authorized an initial issue of insignia (organizational), shoulder sleeve, and nametapes when—

(1) Assigned to a unit.

(2) The command designation is changed.

(3) Reassigned to another command.

c. Initial and replacement nametapes and nameplates are provided at no cost to enlisted members (see AR 670–1).

d. Insignia of rank, nameplates, nametapes, and physical fitness badge will be issued, replaced and attached to enlisted Soldier's ASUs and ACUs at Government expense in the circumstances indicated below:

(1) Promoted to a higher grade.

(2) Reduced in grade.

(3) Conversion to comparable grade.

(4) Authorization and receipt of a supplemental Army uniform.

(5) One Physical Fitness Badge Award under provision of AR 670–1.

e. Insignias purchased from AMCS are attached at the Soldier's expense.

f. Allowances for combat and skill badges are discussed in AR 600–8–22.

g. Attachment of one physical fitness badge to physical fitness clothing is authorized at Government expense for enlisted Soldiers awarded the badge under AR 670–1.

h. Replacement of insignia for enlisted Soldiers will be at Government expense when garments are defective. Normal replacement of insignia and attachment will be at the Soldier's expense.

i. Attachment of insignia is an installation or unit responsibility. Suggested methods include but are not limited to the use of local maintenance facility or company, local off post contractor, or the Exchange concessionaire. Local procedures will be developed.

5–6. Reserve Component Soldiers ordered to initial active duty for training

a. Enlisted Soldiers ordered to IADT are provided all necessary clothing listed in CTA 50–900, as appropriate, in the quantities shown in the "AA–P" column upon arrival at the training site.

b. Commanders of ARNG and USAR Soldiers who enlist more than 60 days before IADT may elect to issue one uniform consisting of the following:

(1) One ACU uniform (coat and trousers).

(2) One desert-sand colored riggers belt.

(3) One pair of combat boots (hot weather or temperate).

(4) Three pairs of socks

(5) One ACU patrol cap.

(6) One duffel bag.

(7) Two sand-colored, moisture wicking T-shirts.

c. When required by seasonal and weather conditions, the following additional items may be issued:

(1) One pair of gloves (utility green) and one pair of glove inserts.

(2) One additional ACU may be issued when authorized by the State Adjutant General.

(3) Combat boots are issued only in new condition, Condition Code A.

(4) Other items may be issued from serviceable stocks of the ARNG or USAR.

(5) The Extended Cold Weather Clothing System Generation II Parka, will be issued as OCIE, per AR 710–2.

d. When ARNG or USAR Soldiers are ordered to IADT, commanders will ensure Soldiers have their personal clothing record and all previously issued clothing under provisions of paragraph 5–6*b* in their possession when reporting to the training site. The commander will annotate the clothing record with one of the following, as appropriate:

(1) "Soldier in possession of clothing records and has not been issued clothing."
(2) "Soldier has not been issued clothing prior to IADT."
(3) "Soldier in possession of clothing records and has been issued a partial issue of clothing."

e. Commanders of USAR or ARNG personnel participating in split-option training will ensure that a copy of their clothing record, DA Form 4886 and all clothing previously issued accompanies the Soldier returning to training site for subsequent training.

f. Upon completion of the initial training period under the split option program, the Soldier returns to the assigned reserve component unit for normal drills. Commanders will not withdraw those items issued in excess of reserve component allowances as discussed in paragraph 12–5.

g. USAR commanders will ensure that newly assigned enlisted nonprior service Soldiers ordered to IADT are prepared, processed, and forwarded to the CCDF during the initial in processing.

h. Instructions for filling out the DA Form 3078 are outlined in paragraph 1–6*p*.

i. If DA Form 3078 is submitted between drill assemblies, unit commanders will delegate approval authority on memorandum to an available officer or warrant officer. A copy of the memorandum and current copy of DA Form 7000 will be forwarded to AMCS.

(1) DA Forms 3078 will contain only those personal items and quantities according to paragraph 5–6*b*, and stamped or annotated "Nonprior service Expedite" prior to forwarding to the AMCS.
(2) AMCS will process the DA Form 3078 by priority.

5–7. Reserve Component Soldiers ordered to extended active duty

a. Enlisted Soldiers ordered to active duty within 3 months of previous release from active duty must report for duty with all clothing in their possession at the time of their release or discharge.

b. Enlisted Soldiers ordered to extended active duty after 3 months from date of release from previous active duty, or those with no previous active duty, must report for duty with all items of clothing recorded on their personal clothing record. This record is sent from their reserve unit to the new active duty station. The use of the personal clothing record is discontinued during the extended active duty.

(1) Clothing in the possession of the enlisted Soldier is inspected to determine serviceability and shortages.
(a) Unserviceable but repairable items are repaired at Government expense.
(b) Unserviceable, uneconomically repairable items are replaced at Government expense.
(c) Shortages are replaced at the expense of the Soldier if the shortages occurred through fault or neglect on the part of the enlisted Soldier.
(2) ARNG and USAR unit commanders will request clothing from the CCDF, using the procedures specified in the ARNG CCD User Handbook.
(3) When on active duty, all enlisted Soldiers begin to accrue basic clothing replacement allowance on completion of 6 months of active duty service in a pay status. Personnel officers or the custodian of the Soldier's financial data record folder will process the necessary pay orders. Accrual of the basic allowance starts on the date after completing 6 months (180 days) of active duty in a pay status.

5–8. Clothing for prisoners in Army confinement facility

a. Temporary issues. Prisoners who are in an undetermined status and confined with the minimum clothing prescribed by the confinement facility are given a temporary issue of clothing, if necessary and where available. Prisoners traveling to a correctional facility may wear personal civilian clothing; however, a temporary issue of comfort clothing may be authorized if required. All military clothing will be inventoried for serviceability to determine if temporary issue will be required.

(1) The installation commander is authorized to maintain minimum quantities of used clothing items at the confinement facility. The service stock listing of Army uniforms with components must be approved by the Army command or major Army subcommand commander. Temporary issues may be withdrawn and clothing reissued, whenever possible.

(2) The commander at the installation where the individual is being held will immediately determine the status of the prisoner. At the earliest possible date, clothing will be furnished to an Army prisoner as authorized in this regulation (see table 5–3).

Table 5–3
Clothing requirement for prisoners in Army correctional or confinement facilities

Personal clothing items	Male	Female
Bag, duffel	—	—
Belt, trousers	1	1
Boot, combat	1	1
Buckle, black	1	1
Buckle, brass	1	—
Cap, patrol ACU	2	2
Cap, synthetic micro	1	1
Coat, all weather	1	1
Coat, ACU	2	2
Coat, CW	1	1
Coat, poly/wool ASU	1	1
Coat, all weather double breasted	1	1
Drawers, brown	7	—
Glove, utility	1	1
Glove, inserts	2	2
Handbag	—	1
Necktab, long/short sleeve	—	1 ea
Necktie	1	—
Skirt, long/short sleeve	—	1
Shoes, oxford	1	1 ea
Necktie, man's black	1	0
Skirt, long/short sleeve	1 ea	1 ea
Shoes, oxford	1	1
Skirt, poly/wool AB 450	—	1
Slacks, poly/wool AB 451	—	1
Socks, cotton/nylon	3	—
Socks, wool	3	3
Towel, bath	2	2
Trousers, ACU	2	2
Trousers, poly/wool AB	1	—
Undershirt, sand	7	7
Undershirt, white	2	—

Notes:

[1] Three sets of undergarments may be issued to enlisted women as necessary. Sentenced prisoners will wear prisoner clothing prescribed by the facility in which they are confined. Appropriate attire other than the prisoner uniforms will be temporarily issued and worn for appearance at court-martial and other appropriate occasions.

[2] Individuals being transferred to a detainment or confinement facility without personal clothing will be issued clothing items, as necessary, at final destination.

[3] Distinctive clothing for prisoners confined at the U.S. Disciplinary Barracks (USDB) will be furnished at the facility.

[4] Members of other Services confined at the USDB will be issued required prisoner clothing.

[5] Soldiers transferred to USDB will not be required to report with all initial issued items. Commanders may transfer the Soldier in civilian clothing, if available. Otherwise a Service uniform will be provided as a temporary issue.

Table 5–4
Clothing required for prisoners in Army correctional and/or confinement facilities, pretrial and/or casual confinement status (temporary issue)

Organizational items	Male	Female
Bag barracks	1	1
Seasonal items	Male	Female
Drawers CW	1	1
Undershirt CW	1	1

(3) After the installation commander determines the status of the prisoner and clothing is issued, any part of the temporary issue that is recoverable is withdrawn, laundered, and retained by the facility officer for reissue. Footwear and other nonrecoverable items are retained by and charged against the Army enlisted Soldier, per paragraph 4–3b(4) or 4–3b(5). Footwear issued to other than Army prisoners is withdrawn and returned to supply channels for proper disposition.

(4) Footwear is issued to other than Army prisoners only when the prisoner does not have footwear to perform assigned duties.

(5) Clothing temporarily provided to prisoners, other than Army, is without reimbursement from the member or from their military Service. Army clothing is withdrawn as soon as clothing is obtained from the prisoner's Service.

b. Responsibility for issue. The commander of units where Army prisoners are assigned will ensure that the prisoner has at all times required clothing items (see table 5–3). The correctional officer is responsible for prisoners of the other Services. Soldiers who are returned to military custody at other than home stations and who are detained in a confinement or non-confinement status pending disposition are given a temporary issue of clothing if necessary (except nonrecoverable items). Soldiers without an ASU may be given a temporary issue of these items, if they are to appear before courts or elimination boards.

c. Regular issues.

(1) *Army prisoners.* The commander of the correctional holding detachment, special processing detachment, or other units where prisoners are assigned ensures that during pretrial or post trial confinement, each Army prisoner has the items required by the facility. Prisoners receiving a basic or standard replacement allowance will obtain, if necessary, and maintain prescribed clothing items at their own expense. Prisoners are required to have all clothing authorizations in their possession on arrival at the confinement facility for incarceration (see table 5–3). Replacement of clothing shortages will be at the expense of the prisoner, if the prisoners are receiving pay and the clothing replacement allowance.

(2) *Other than Army prisoners.* Casual prisoners of other Services are provided temporary issues as required. After the status of the prisoner is determined, the prisoner's Service is notified to provide adequate clothing for the Soldier's return trip to home station. Prisoners confined in Army confinement facilities pending court-martial or serving their sentence will be provided a complete allowance of clothing as authorized in DODI 1325.07.

5–9. Initial issue to prisoners restored to duty

Prisoners restored to duty are issued initial allowances before departure for duty assignment per paragraph 4–2c. The USDB is excluded. Prisoners at the USDB are given a seasonal Army Service Uniform. Initial allowances are completed at the new duty station if the Soldier does not elect to go on leave. This authorization does not apply to prisoners who have no punitive discharge and who continued to receive a CRA while in confinement.

5–10. Clothing for prisoners detained in personnel control facilities

a. A personnel control facility (PCF) is authorized to stock minimum quantities of clothing and footwear for temporary issues to detained personnel (see table 5–3 for description of clothing items and the quantities). Prisoners awaiting discharge will receive a temporary issue of clothing required for performing duty at the facility. This clothing will be withdrawn when the prisoner is discharged. Prisoners of the PCF awaiting reassignment will be issued clothing to complete their CB authorization. This issue will be at the Soldier's expense. The PCF commanders will make every effort to obtain Condition Code B clothing prior to ordering new items through the installation supply division (ISD). Clothing ordered by the PCF will be charged to the OMA fund. The ISD will order on an as-required basis and will not accumulate demand data for the purpose of replenishing clothing to support the PCF. Authority will be obtained from local medical authorities for the sanitation and reissue of footwear and undergarments.

b. Personnel will be required to return all clothing when discharged from the Service. Those Soldiers returned to military control in a pay status will be charged for all clothing retained. See paragraph 5–14 for those in a nonpay status. Undergarments for female personnel are not stocked in the supply system; therefore the purchases of these garments will be charged to OMA funds.

5–11. Exchange or alteration of misfit clothing and footwear

a. Exchanges or alteration of misfit clothing and footwear after initial issue must be made within 6 months (180 days) of date of entitlement. By definition, exchanges are to replace one like item with another; therefore, AMCS must accept another garment or footwear item when making exchange transactions.

b. Exchange of misfit footwear after initial issue must be made within 90 days of issue.

c. When the unit commander decides that clothing or footwear is actually a misfit, the supply sergeant or specialist will prepare and submit the DA Form 3078 as outlined in paragraph 1–6p.

d. Hard-copy submissions will be properly prepared in original and three copies. A statement will be placed in block 30, "Remarks," giving an explanation for exchange. Use of a single DA Form 3078 to permit exchange of clothing items for more than one Soldier is authorized for basic trainees when exchange is accomplished at CIIP. A DA Form 3078 otherwise is required for each enlisted Soldier. Place a check in the "Exchange" block of the form. The following information is required:

(1) A list of the items of clothing or footwear.

(2) A statement on the front of the form or in the remarks block that the enlisted Soldier has been in the Service for fewer than 6 months (180 days) or 90 days, for the exchange of footwear, after the last authorization of an initial allowance. Give the day, month, and year of entry on duty.

e. When forms are completed, the unit commander will have the enlisted Soldier—

(1) Go to the AMCS or CIIP. When a CIIP is located on an installation, the commander should use the CIIP.

(2) Present the applicable number of copies of DA Form 3078 to the AMCS associate. The associate in turn has a qualified clothing or shoe fitter check the fit of the clothing or footwear.

f. If the garments can be fitted by alteration, the fitter marks the alterations. The garments are then sent to the alteration shop and upon completion are returned to the enlisted Soldier. If some garments on the same DA Form 3078 cannot be fitted by alterations, these items should be exchanged for an appropriate size. If exchanged garments require alterations mark the issue column of DA Form 3078, "Alter" for any garments that can be altered. Follow procedures in paragraph 5–11g for all other items. If all garments listed on the form can be altered, destroy DA Form 3078.

g. Misfit clothing that cannot be altered to achieve the proper fit and misfit footwear is turned in to the AMCS or CIIP without additional documentation. The correct size clothing or footwear is issued and recorded on DA Form 3078. First issue priority for exchanges will be from available Condition Code B, 75 percent wear (used) clothing. The duplicate copy is returned to the unit commander for destruction. The AMCS or CIIP processes the original and one copy of the DA Form 3078 for financial accounting.

h. If the proper size garment is out of stock at the time requested, enter zero in the "Issue" column of DA Form 3078. Return a duplicate copy of DA Form 3078 to the unit commander for filing until the exchange for the proper size is made. Send a duplicate of DA Form 3078 to the new station if the enlisted Soldier is transferred before the exchange is made. This copy is authority to exchange misfit items when the proper size is available, even though the initial (180 days) 6-month period of service may have elapsed. Destroy this copy when the exchange is made. The misfit clothing is turned in when the proper size is available.

i. Items exchanged must be cleaned, pressed and meet the Condition Code B standards; otherwise an exchange will not be made.

j. Those enlisted Soldiers in the split training option program will be entitled to exchanges and alterations during the second phase of IADT.

k. For exchanges made at AMCS, removal and reattachment of insignia will be accomplished through the alteration facility at no charge to Soldier.

5–12. Exchanges of clothing for reasons other than misfit

a. During the first 6 months (180 days) of active duty, which includes basic and advanced individual training, exchanges may be made when items of personal clothing are damaged beyond repair incident to service or intensive training and not due to normal FWT. This is provided such damage was not caused by any fault or negligence on the part of the Soldier. A mismatched ACU set—that is the trousers and coat do not match in color or shades—is not a legitimate reason for exchange.

b. The replacement of clothing or footwear damaged during participation in field training exercises, regardless of time in service, is not authorized. Soldiers will be issued protective clothing authorized by CTA 50–900 when working in areas such as welding or performing such tasks as handling batteries. Commanders will also consider the use of code X clothing (less than Condition Code B) in lieu of normal work uniforms when situations warrant.

c. The unit supply sergeant or specialist will prepare and submit the DA Form 3078 as outlined in paragraph 1–6p and place a statement in block 30, "Remarks," giving an explanation for the exchange.

d. Items turned in for exchange under this paragraph will be in a clean condition and have no salable value. The AMCS will not take these items into their accountability but will turn them in to the local DLA Disposition Services at no value. Authorized items, accepted for exchanges that are not taken into AMCS accountability will not be charged to the write off account 109–13. The CIIP will follow normal turn-in procedures.

e. Items that have obvious defects in workmanship or material will be handled as follows:

(1) Repairs at Government expense are authorized if it is economical to repair the item, and if the repairs would not cause a visible defect.

(2) Items returned to the issue activity that cannot be economically repaired will be accepted for exchange. The CIIP or AMCS manager will submit SF 368.

f. Items received under paragraph 5–12*e*(2) will be exchanged using DA Form 3078 as outlined in paragraph 5–11. For CIIP, the defective item will be turned in to the supporting ISD and will be processed under dollar value accountability. AMCS will make turn-ins in accordance with EOP 40–4.

g. For exchanges made at AMCS, removal and reattachment of insignia will be accomplished through the alteration facility at no charge to the Soldier.

5–13. Initial and gratuitous issues to Soldiers isolated from supporting installations

When enlisted Soldiers are isolated from the installation where they are based for support, the assigned installation commander will process initial and gratuitous issues as follows:

a. Initial issue. Personal clothing items, when required to complete initial allowances, are obtained from the AMCS of the installation providing support.

b. Gratuitous issue. Gratuitous issues are processed as indicated in paragraph 5–4.

c. Submission of form. DA Form 3078 is submitted only to the supporting installation.

5–14. Nonpay status

a. When enlisted Soldiers are in a nonpay status, an issue of clothing is authorized, if necessary. Individual charge sales will not be prepared for clothing issues for individuals in a nonpay status. Clothing ordered will be chargeable to OMA funds and through normal supply channels.

b. Serviceable recoverable items will be withdrawn when the issue of clothing is no longer required by the Soldier. Commanders of units other than confinement or control facilities will turn in withdrawn serviceable clothing to the ISD.

5–15. Reenlistments

a. Enlisted Soldiers who have 3 or fewer years of active duty service at the time of discharge or release and who reenlist within 3 months (90 days) are entitled to an issue-in-kind of like items turned in at time of discharge per paragraph 12–2. Requests for items not required for turn-in are substantiated by valid proof of turn-in or are replaced at the Soldier's expense.

b. Persons who have more than 3 years of active duty service at the time of discharge or release and who reenlisted within 3 months (90 days) are not entitled to an issue-in-kind of any personal clothing items. The Soldier retains such items per paragraph 12–2.

Chapter 6
Clothing Initial Issue Point

6–1. Introduction

a. Procedures may be modified, if necessary, to adapt to automation. This includes DA Form 3078 and DA Form 4886 more suitable to the automated system. However, the automated system must meet these requirements to establish effective internal accounting control.

b. The CIIPs are staffed and operated under the guidelines for base operation support. TRADOC's goal is to clothe each Soldier with 100 percent of their authorized clothing allowance as stated in CTA 50–900. Clothing and footwear will be fitted in accordance with TM 10–227 prior to the Soldier leaving the CIIP installation. During periods in which clothing shortages may be prevalent, this goal may not be attainable. If 100 percent of the clothing bag items are not issued during the initial processing, commanders will make every possible effort to obtain needed clothing for the Soldier. Only DLA–TS procured clothing items will be issued to new recruits. Requests (memorandum) for exception to this policy must be submitted to the DCS, G–4 (DALO–SUI) for approval. Clothing forms (DA Form 3078) will not be destroyed until 100 percent of all authorized issues have been made and the Soldiers reach their initial permanent duty stations. DA Form 3078 will be retained for RC personnel per paragraph 12–5*c*.

6–2. Concept of operations

a. The inventory in the CIIPs is owned by DLA–TS. The overall management for CIIP operations, to include ownership and maintenance of all buildings, equipment, and personnel falls under base operations procedures. Policy and procedures associated with the CIIP issuance of clothing are coordinated among TRADOC, the DCS, G–4 (DALO–SUI), and the CIIP.

b. Actual operation of CIIPs is assigned to an individual designated as the manager or officer in charge of the activity.

c. The property control officer is normally accountable for the inventories in the CIIP.

d. DLA–TS has designated the CIIP inventory as DLA–TS depot assets. Transfer of stock between CIIP sites will be as directed by DLA–TS.

e. Adjustments to the CIIP account will be in accordance with DLA guidance and operating procedures. Adjustments include, but are not limited to, price changes and inventory adjustments.

f. Funds to operate CIIPs will be obtained through the responsible operating command.

6–3. Establishment

a. Normally, CIIP facilities are established at installations operating reception stations designated for this mission.

b. CIIPs may also be established at OCONUS replacement centers and at Army personnel processing centers. The Army commander concerned determines the need for such facilities.

6–4. Inventories

a. Formal inventories are taken twice a year with at least 4 months between inventories as follows:

(1) DLA determines the procedures and times of the inventories.

(2) When a new manager or officer in charge is appointed.

(3) Informal inventories are taken as required between formal scheduled inventories. These inventories are taken to determine the condition of the account and the losses, gains, errors, price changes, and replenishments.

b. Facilities may be closed for a period not to exceed 3 workdays when formal inventories are made.

6–5. Inventory and operations

a. All CIIPs will maintain stocks of complete tariff sizes of CB items and footwear (see Supply Bulletin (SB) 10–523).

b. Items of OCIE, which normally accompany the Soldier on transfer, may be stocked and issued through the CIIP.

(1) Items of OCIE issued to Soldiers may be temporarily recorded on DA Form 3078. A machine-produced equivalent, approved by the ACOM, may be used in lieu of DA Form 3078. The DA Form 3078 will be retained until the Soldier completes 6 months (180 days) of service, has been issued a complete allowance of personal clothing items, or has in-processed at their initial permanent duty station, whichever date is later.

(2) When in-processing at initial permanent duty station, all OCIE issued during reception center processing will be transferred to DA Form 3645 (Organizational Clothing and Individual Equipment Record) (see DA Pam 710–2–1 for OCIE property book procedures). All future issues and turn-ins of OCIE made to Soldiers will be recorded on the Soldier's DA Form 3645.

c. ASU coats, skirts, slacks and trousers that are not free of wrinkles will be pressed prior to try-on and issue.

d. All footwear and outer garments will be tried on and fitted while the individual is wearing proper subgarments. For proper fitting of uniforms and footwear, see TM 10–227 or TRADOC standard operating procedures for CIIPs.

e. Required alterations will be made within 5 days.

f. Only authorized alterations will be made.

g. No alteration will be made that will change the approved concept of fit.

h. Requirements for special measurement clothing or footwear are discussed in chapter 7 of this regulation.

6–6. Physical layout and processing

a. Efficiency in operation can best be obtained through a self-contained facility that has areas for—

(1) Adequate storage space.

(2) Orientation and disrobing.

(3) Recording physical measurements.

(4) Providing an orderly sequence of issuing initial allowances of clothing.

(5) Providing a final check of items issued, alterations made, and pressing performed.

b. The CIIP will be attractive and provide individual services to favorably impress the new Soldier.

c. An orientation on the clothing issue procedures and the mechanics of the clothing monetary allowance system will precede the recording of body measurements (see chap 4). Proper fitting and wearing of the uniform will be emphasized. Before arrival at the CIIP, Soldiers to be processed will be freshly showered and provided haircuts.

d. The importance of proper fitting of uniforms and footwear must be stressed, rather than processing at a high rate. Showing training films on fitting Army uniforms and footwear is encouraged for maximum use of on the job training. Issue sequence will be established locally. The Soldier must ensure they are in receipt of all items recorded on DA Form 3078 as being issued. After completion of issues, the individual will sign all copies of DA Form 3078.

e. An issue may be provided at the time the Soldier reports to the reception station. Issue normally will be limited to items that do not require fitting (towels, underwear, socks, and duffel bag).

f. Processing time will provide for the following:

(1) Selecting initial try-on sizes from recorded physical measurements.

(2) Trying on additional sizes, if necessary, to ensure the best possible fit with the least alterations.

(3) Furnishing the Soldier with a receipt for garments withdrawn for alterations.

(4) Recording the quantity issued.

g. Soldiers will not sign DA Form 3078 until they have been issued clothing marked in ISS column.

h. Exchanges for misfit garments (see para 5–11) and damaged items (see para 5–12*a*), will be accomplished within established time frames as can be scheduled and processed.

i. If a Soldier does not meet requirements of TM 10–227 prior to departure from initial entry training, misfit exchange will be accomplished.

6–7. Alteration facilities

Alteration facilities will be established at each CIIP. There must be enough equipment to ensure that all clothing issued to Soldiers is altered to achieve proper fit. The facilities of established clothing and equipment repair shops or contractual alteration vendors will be used to make alterations. DD Form 754 (Repair Tag) is authorized for use. Alteration of all clothing is charged to OMA funds. For fitting of uniforms see paragraph 2–5. For quality control of uniform see paragraph 2–6.

Chapter 7
Special Measurement Clothing and Footwear

7–1. Special measurement clothing

Special measurement clothing items are manufactured to the specific measurements of a person. These items are authorized only for Soldiers who cannot be properly fitted with standard tariff sizes or by authorized alterations. Unless directed otherwise, Soldiers take all special measurement clothing with them on permanent change of station moves. Retired personnel are not provided special measurement clothing.

7–2. Procedures for supply of special measurement clothing

a. If a Soldier cannot be fitted from tariff sizes or by authorized alterations at the time of initial issue or sale, they may be measured for special measurement clothing. The measurements are recorded on DD Form 358 (Armed Forces Measurement Blank-Special Sized Clothing for Men) or DD Form 1111 (Armed Forces Measurement Blank-Special Sized Clothing for Women). See AR 32–4. ARNG requirements may be ordered using the automated process specified in the CCD User Handbook.

b. The CIIP prepares DD Form 358 and DD Form 1111 in quadruplicate and sends them to the ISD. In turn, the ISD prepares DD Form 1348–6. The name of the Soldier for whom special measurements form is attached and a description of item ordered is entered in the remarks column of the form.

(1) The originals of DD Form 1348 and either DD Form 358 or DD Form 1111 are submitted to the Commander, DLA–TS (DLA–TS–FRC) (Room 310), 700 Robbins Avenue, Philadelphia, PA 19111–5092. Requisition priority 06 is used for requests for initial issue clothing for new Soldiers per AR 725–50.

(2) The supply officer retains one copy of DD Form 1348–6 and one copy of the special measurement form.

c. Two copies of the special measurement form are annotated to show the assigned requisition number. One copy is returned to the preparing activity. The supply officer sends the other copy to the commander of the Soldier being fitted. This copy is then filed with the Soldier's assigned unit. It is destroyed when the item is received. Follow-up action is maintained on the supply status until the transaction is completed and items are received.

d. AMCS personnel prepare DD Form 358 and DD Form 1111 per EOP 40–4. When items are received, the AMCS or CIIP notifies the Soldier's commander that the items are available. The unit supply sergeant or specialist prepares a DA Form 3078 as outlined in paragraph 1–6*p* when the items are to be issued. For a hard copy submission, include the original and four copies.

e. If the Soldier is transferred before the items requisitioned are received, the following actions are necessary.

(1) The Soldier's commander furnishes a copy of the transfer orders to the AMCS or CIIP.

(2) The AMCS or CIIP immediately—

(a) Advises the Commander, DLA–TS of the new address of the Soldier.

(b) Cites the correct requisition number.

(c) Requests the clothing be forwarded to the Soldier's new location.

(3) The Commander, DLA–TS immediately advises the AMCS or CIIP whether or not the change can be made.

(4) If the clothing is received at the station after the Soldier is transferred, the AMCS or CIIP ships the items to the

AMCS of the new station by the most expeditious means. A copy of the order transferring the Soldier is sent with the items.

(5) If the DA Form 3078 indicates non-receipt of special measurement items, the Soldier's commander immediately notifies the AMCS or CIIP. The notification will initiate a follow-up action and resubmission of a special measurement requisition for the same item or items can be prevented.

f. If items are received after the Soldier is honorably discharged or relieved from active duty, they are advised that the items are available and can be purchased within 60 days. If the Soldier does not wish to buy the items within the 60 days, items are processed for turn in.

7–3. Special measurement footwear

a. Special measurement footwear consists of boots or shoes that must be manufactured for size only. These items are not included in regular sizes stocked in the depot system. Rather, they are manufactured to a Soldier's specific measurement. Special measurement footwear is included under the clothing replacement system. Retired personnel are not provided special measurement footwear.

b. These items of footwear are authorized only for Soldiers who cannot be properly fitted from standard tariff sizes. Unless directed otherwise, Soldiers take all special measurement footwear with them on permanent change of station moves.

c. Commanders of ACOMs may approve the issue or sale of authorized allowances of combat boots and shoes to active duty Soldiers with mismatched feet to ensure a proper fit of both feet. Soldiers will pay the current standard price of only one pair of such footwear. The Army CIIP or AMCS issuing or selling this special footwear is authorized to dispose of the remaining unused footwear through DRMS channels.

7–4. Procedures for supply of special measurement footwear

a. Soldiers who cannot be fitted properly with regular tariff sizes of footwear are sent to the local medical facility. A member of the medical office prepares a DD Form 150 (Special Measurements Blank for Special Measurements/Orthopedic Boots and Shoes), in quadruplicate. The form is forwarded to the AMCS, who prepares a DD Form 1348–6 (DOD Single Line Item Requisition System Document (Manual-Long Form)) in quadruplicate, for the Soldier for a trial pair of special measurement footwear (see AR 32–4). When both low quarter shoes and combat boots are required, the combat boots are the trial pair. The name of the Soldier and the type of footwear are annotated in the remarks column of the requisition.

(1) Original copies of DD Form 1348-6 and DD Form 150 are mailed to Veterans Integrated Service Network, 3 Department of Veterans Affairs Medical Center (Network Prosthetics), 423 East 23rd Street, New York, NY 10010–5011.

(2) The AMCS retains two copies of DD Form 150 and DD Form 1348–6.

(3) The assigned requisition number is annotated on two copies of DD Form 150. One copy is sent to the unit commander of the Soldier requesting for special measurement footwear.

b. The AMCS manager arranges an appointment between the Soldier and the local medical facility on receipt of the trial pair of boots and fitting report from the Veterans Administration. The fitting report must be kept with the footwear. The medical officer decides if the footwear fits properly and completes the fitting report as follows:

(1) If the footwear does not fit, the medical officer records all changes required on the fitting report. They return the reports and footwear to the AMCS manager. The fitting report and the trial pair of footwear are returned to the Veterans Administration for correction and returned to AMCS.

(2) If the trial pair fits properly, the medical officer completes the fitting report and forwards it to the AMCS manager. The AMCS manager completes the issue or sale as prescribed in paragraphs 3–6 and 5–3.

c. After the trial pair is fitted properly, the AMCS prepares a requisition for the balance of the footwear authorized for issue to or requested for purchase by the Soldier. The requisition is sent with the fitting report to the Defense Orthopedic Footwear Clinic.

d. On receipt of the remaining footwear and later deliveries of replacement special measurement footwear, the procedures in paragraph 7–4b apply. When the issue or sale is complete, the annotated DD Form 150 is forwarded to the unit for filing per AR 25–400–2.

e. When replacement footwear is needed, the Soldier reports to the AMCS with the copy of DD Form 150. The AMCS refers the Soldier to a medical facility to decide if the Soldier's foot measurements have changed. If measurements have changed, a new DD Form 150 marked "revised" is prepared. This form is sent with the requisition. Otherwise, replacement footwear is requisitioned with a statement that the previously requisitioned measurements are satisfactory. The original DD Form 150 or a copy of the new revised form is annotated to show the requisition number. The form is sent to the Soldier's unit for retention.

f. The AMCS manager ensures DD Form 150 is forwarded promptly to the Veterans Administration.

g. When a Soldier is transferred before items requisitioned are received, or the Soldier has been honorably discharged or relieved from active duty, the procedures in paragraphs 7–2e and 7–2f apply. The Veterans Administration is notified of the Soldiers' new duty station.

h. Pricing policy for special measurement clothing and footwear is contained in paragraph 3–4.

7–5. Prices of special measurement clothing and footwear
a. The DOD EMALL standard prices for special measurement clothing and footwear for enlisted Soldier will be adjusted and issued or sold at no additional cost.

b. The DOD EMALL standard prices for special measurement clothing and footwear will be adjusted and officers will procure items using personal funds.

7–6. Supply of orthopedic footwear
Orthopedic footwear is a medical appliance and is obtained through medical supply channels from the Veterans Administration (see AR 32–4 and AR 40–3).

Chapter 8
Civilian Clothing

8–1. Introduction
a. This chapter implements 37 USC 418 and 37 USC 419 and DOD instruction (DODI) 1338.18, which provides policy for the officer and enlisted civilian-clothing allowance (CCA). Service members directed by competent authority to dress in civilian clothing more than half the time when performing official duty, as a military requirement, are eligible to apply for a CCA. Officers can apply only if they are assigned active duty outside the United States, or perform temporary duty (TDY) outside the United States from an OCONUS assignment (see para 8–2b). Enlisted Soldiers who are on extended active duty assigned within or outside the United States are eligible to apply for a CCA (see para 8–2a). This includes classified duties. However, this does not include enlisted Soldiers or officers who are discharged from the Service upon release from confinement and whose punitive sentences have been executed.

b. The enlisted and officer CCA program applies to USAR or ARNG personnel on orders to active duty over 179 days.

c. Further information may be obtained from Commander, U.S. Army Human Resources Command (AHRC–ALL–S), 1600 Spearhead Division Avenue, Fort Knox, KY, 40121–5205.

8–2. Who may receive allowances
a. Enlisted Soldiers. When performing official duty more than half the time and when approved by their Army Command as a military requirement, enlisted Soldiers may be authorized a civilian allowance. Enlisted Soldiers are eligible to receive a CCA when reporting on a permanent change of station to an OCONUS location. Enlisted Soldiers may receive payment of that allowance 90 days prior to their report date as stated on their orders. See points of contact list in table 8–1, for enlisted Soldiers to contact when assigned within or outside the United States and who are—

(1) On duty at the White House. The military aide decides whether civilian clothing is necessary or suitable.

(2) Performing congressional escort duties. The Chief, Legislative Liaison decides whether civilian clothing is necessary or suitable.

(3) Assigned to intelligence, security, or related activities clearly requiring civilian clothing be worn.

(4) Assigned to permanent or temporary duty in a foreign country where the host-nation government prohibits U.S. military personnel from wearing their military uniform, as noted in the DODD 4500.54E.

(5) Assigned or attached to Army attaché offices. The DCS, G–2 decides whether civilian clothing is necessary.

(6) Assigned to Military Assistance Advisory Group (MAAG) activities. The Chief of MAAG decides whether civilian clothing is necessary (see AR 1–75).

(7) Assigned to an explosive ordnance disposal unit to protect the President and other high-ranking officials.

(8) Assigned to duty in support of U.S. Secret Service Protective Missions and explosive detector dog handlers.

(9) Assigned to a law enforcement activity, military police investigator (MPI) office, or the U.S. Army Criminal Investigation Command.

b. Officers. By law, an officer is authorized a CCA only if the officer's permanent duty station is outside the United States. Officers who are eligible to receive a CCA and are reporting on a permanent change of station to an OCONUS location may receive payment of that allowance 90 days prior to their report date as stated on their orders. See the point of contact list in table 8–1 for officers to contact when assigned outside the United States who are—

(1) Assigned to permanent or temporary duty in a foreign country where the host-nation government prohibits U.S. military personnel from wearing their military uniform, as noted in the DODD 4500.54E.

(2) Assigned outside the United States to intelligence, security, or related activities clearly requiring civilian clothing be worn.

(3) Assigned OCONUS or attached to Army attaché offices to include foreign area officer in country trainees. The DCS, G–2 decides whether civilian clothing is necessary.

(4) Assigned outside the United States to MAAG activities. The Chief of MAAG decides whether civilian clothing is necessary (see AR 1–75).

c. Training with industry program. Officer and enlisted Soldiers in the TWI program do not qualify for CCA per Army policy.

Table 8–1
Authorized points of contacts at Army command level

Command	Address
AFRICOM	Commander U.S. Africa Command (Commandant's Office) Unit 29951 APO, AE 09751–9951
AMC	Commander U.S. Army Materiel Command AMCPE–MPD 9301 Chapek Rd. Fort Belvoir, VA 22060–5527
ARCYBER	Commander U.S. Army Cyber Command 8825 Beulah Street (ARCC–CG) Fort Belvoir, VA 22060–5246
ARSOUTH	Commander U.S. Army South (ARSO–LGS) 4130 Stanley Road, Suite 201 Fort Sam Houston, TX 78234–5100
ATEC	Headquarters U.S. Army Test and Evaluation Command 4501 Ford Avenue Alexandria, VA 22302–1458
CENTCOM	Commander U.S. Central Command (CCJ1–MPAR) MacDill AFB, FL 33621–5101
CIDC	Commander U.S. Army Criminal Investigation Command (CISP–PE–AC) 27130 Telegraph Road Quantico, VA 22134-2253
EUCOM	Commander U.S. European Command (CCS–HC) Unit 30400 P.O. Box 1000 APO AE 09131–4209
EUSA	Commander Eighth Army (EAGA–PSC 303) APO AP 06205
FORSCOM	Commander U.S. Army Forces Command (AFLG–SMS) Fort Bragg, NC 28310–5000
MEDCOM	Commander U.S. Army Medical Command (MCPE–MA) 2050 Worth Road, Suite 7 Fort Sam Houston, TX 78234–6007

Table 8–1
Authorized points of contacts at Army command level—Continued

Command	Address
IMCOM	Commander U.S. Army Installation Management Command (CFIM–HR) 2405 Gunshed Road Fort Sam Houston, TX 78234–1223
INSCOM	Commander U.S. Army Intelligence and Security Command (IAPE–MP–P) 8825 Beulah Street Fort Belvoir, VA 22060–5246
MDW	Commander U.S. Army Military District of Washington (ANPE–SFS) 103 3rd Avenue SW Bldg. 39 Fort McNair, Washington, DC 20319–5058
NETCOM/9th SC	Commander U.S. Army Network Enterprise Technology Command SGS SEC General Staff Office NETC–SGS 213 Cushing Street, Suite 3000 Fort Huachuca, AZ 85613–7070
SDDC	Commander Surface Deployment and Distribution Command (SDDC–PL–H–P) Scott Air Force Base, IL 62225
SOUTHCOM	Commander U.S. Southern Command (SCJI–A) 9301 NW 33rd Street Doral, FL 33172–1217
TRADOC	Commander U.S. Army Training and Doctrine Command 210 Dillion Circle (ATBO–H) Fort Eustis, VA 23604
USAE/Supreme Headquarters Allied Powers, Europe (SHAPE)	Commander Headquarters, U.S. Army Element SHAPE (ACOP–P) Unit 21420, Box 5100 APO, AE 09705
USACE	Commander U.S. Army Corps of Engineers (CEHR–M) 441 G. Street, NW Washington DC 20314–1000
USARAF	Commander U.S. Army Africa Unit 31401 BOX 5 APO AE 09630
USARC	Commander U.S. Army Reserve Command 4710 Knox Street Fort Bragg, NC 28310-5010
USARCENT	Commander Third U.S. Army U.S. Army Central Command (ACEN–OSP) Building 1947 1 Gabreski Drive Shaw AFB, SC 29152

Table 8–1
Authorized points of contacts at Army command level—Continued

Command	Address
USAREUR	Commander U.S. Army, Europe (AEALG–SD) Unit 29351 APO AE 09014
USARNORTH	Commander U.S. Army North Command HQ, USARNORTH (5th Army) 1400 East Grayson, Suite 152 Fort Sam Houston, TX 78234–7000
USARPAC	Commander U.S. Army Pacific (APPE–SGM) Fort Shafter, HI 96858–5100
USASMDC/ARTSTAT	Commander U.S. Space and Missile Defense Command/ U.S. Army Forces Strategic Command PO Box 1500 Huntsville, AL 35807-3801
USMA	Commander U.S. Military Academy G–4 (MALO) 646 Swift Road West Point, NY 10996
USPACOM	Commander U.S. Pacific Command APPA–J6 Building T100 Fort Shafter, HI 96858–5100
USSOCOM	Commander U.S. Special Operations Command J1–PA MacDill AFB, FL 33621

8–3. Who may approve allowances

Officers and enlisted Soldiers who are required to wear civilian clothing more than half of the time when performing official duty and who desire a CCA will ask their unit commander to create the written justification required per paragraph 8–5. The unit commander will forward the request to the applicable point of contact for approval. Approval authority for a CCA may not be further delegated below the organizations listed in table 8–1. The following type of requests requires special handling.

   a. Requests for officer and enlisted criminal investigation division special agents are sent from the Soldier's unit commander to Commander, U.S. Army Criminal Investigation Command (CISP–PE–AC), 6010 6th Street, Fort Belvoir, VA 22060–5506 for verification and approval authority.

   b. Requests for enlisted MPI Soldiers are sent from the Soldier's unit commander to the losing or gaining ACOM point of contact for approval. MPI requests must conform to procedures in AR 190–30.

   c. Requests for officer and enlisted Army attaché Soldiers cannot be submitted until they have officially signed in to INSCOM. Request will be sent from the Soldier's unit commander to the Commander, INSCOM (U.S. Army Field Support Center) (IAPE–MP), Fort George G. Meade, MD 20755–5905, for verification of attaché status prior to the ACOM point of contact for approval.

   d. Classified requests for a CCA must be processed using secure means from the Soldier's unit commander to the gaining ACOM for approval.

   e. Requests for officers performing Foreign Area Officer duties must be forwarded through the appropriate supporting personnel officer at either Fort George G. Meade, MD; Fort Shafter, HI; or U.S. Army Security Assistance Agency, Latin America at Fort Buchanan, PR, prior to the applicable command approval (see table 8–1).

8–4. Types and quantities of allowances

The type of assignments or conditions under which civilian clothing may be required can vary. The specific type and quantity of clothing, therefore, cannot be fixed. The clothing, however, will meet the requirements for business, dress, and work of an officer's or enlisted Soldier's assignment. The purchase of items or accessories in quantities that are not needed in performing official duties is not authorized. The rates for a CCA will change at the beginning of each fiscal year on 1 October and will be reflected in the DOD Pay Entitlement Manual. The category of allowance and the criteria for each allowance are listed below:

a. Initial permanent duty civilian clothing allowances. Initial permanent duty CCAs. This allowance is authorized when the enlisted Soldier is initially assigned to a normal tour of permanent duty requiring the full-time wear of civilian clothing or an officer is initially assigned OCONUS to a normal tour of permanent duty requiring the full-time wear of civilian clothing. An initial permanent duty CCA will not be paid more than one time in any 3-year period, or if the member has not been out of a qualifying permanent assignment for less than 12 months. If a member receives a follow-on permanent assignment, they may be eligible for another type of CCA (see para 8–4b). A member who has received a temporary duty CCA within the 12 months of commencing an assignment authorizing a permanent duty CCA will have the permanent duty CCA offset by the applicable prevailing temporary duty CCA (see para 8–3c). As an exception to policy, the ASA (ALT) may authorize a Service to pay the initial CCA and up to two replacement allowance payments in an up-front lump sum to members projected to continue to meet the eligibility criteria for a CCA on a career basis. Such a lump-sum payment will be made only one time in a member's career and that is when the member first becomes eligible for a CCA. On the first and second anniversaries of a lump-sum initial payment, if it is determined that the member will not actually be remaining in a qualifying CCA position for at least the next 6 months, the annual unearned portion for the year(s) not served in a qualifying assignment will be recouped from the member. On the third and subsequent anniversaries of the member being eligible for the allowance, the member will be paid the permanent duty replacement CCA (see para 8–4b).

b. Permanent duty replacement civilian clothing allowance. The permanent duty replacement allowance is equal to 1/3 of the initial permanent duty CCA. The permanent duty replacement CCA is authorized to enlisted Soldiers or officers as indicated below.

(1) On the anniversary month of the member commencing the qualifying assignment, if the member is projected to serve at least 6 additional months in a qualifying permanent duty assignment, a permanent duty replacement CCA will be paid. If the member is projected to remain in the assignment fewer than 6 months beyond the anniversary month, the replacement CCA will not be authorized. However, if the member then actually serves 6 or more months in the assignment past the anniversary month, the replacement allowance will be paid.

(2) If the member receives a follow-on permanent assignment requiring the wear of civilian clothing within 3 years of receiving an initial permanent duty CCA, or within 12 months of occupying a qualifying permanent assignment, the member will continue to be paid the permanent duty replacement CCA on the original anniversary date.

c. Temporary duty civilian clothing allowance. Generally, the TDY CCA is for use when the permanent allowance is not applicable. Officers are eligible to apply if assigned outside the United States. There is only one maximum TDY CCA authorized in a 3-year period. However, in exceptional circumstances, ASA (ALT) may make an exception to this 3-year period rule and authorize an additional payment of TDY CCA. Payment of TDY allowance is not authorized to Soldiers on in transit stopover at locations where civilian clothing must be worn. Neither is the TDY allowance authorized to persons transiting or visiting foreign countries, if TDY is less than 15 days or if for other than "official duty" reasons. Requests for TDY CCAs must meet the provisions of paragraph 8–2 and need strict supervision. Authorizations must not be abused. TDY CCAs are authorized when duty is performed for 15 consecutive or accumulative days or longer (see para 8–2). Reenlistment within 3 months after separation is considered as continuous active duty. In addition, the 15-day consecutive or accumulative qualification requirement does not apply to explosive ordnance disposal and explosive detector dog personnel; these personnel may be authorized up to the maximum TDY CCA for 30 days upon their initial temporary duty travel requirement.

(1) *A temporary duty allowance (15 consecutive or accumulative days or more but fewer than 30 days).* This TDY allowance is authorized to an enlisted Soldier, or officer who is assigned outside the United States, who is required to wear civilian clothing for a TDY period of 15 consecutive or accumulative days or more, but less than 30 days within a 30-day period. As indicated above, this 15-consecutive or accumulative-days requirement does not apply to explosive ordnance disposal and explosive detector dog personnel on U.S. Secret Service Support duty, to Defense Courier Service couriers, or to onsite inspection agency military personnel. The maximum payable for this allowance is 1/3 of the initial permanent duty CCA. Soldiers who receive this allowance because of the length of their TDY and who later perform additional temporary duty within a 3-year period that qualifies them for the maximum TDY payment, are authorized payment of the difference between the two amounts.

(2) *Temporary duty allowance (over 30 days).* This maximum TDY allowance is authorized to enlisted Soldiers, or officers who are assigned outside the United States, who are required to wear civilian clothing for a TDY period of more than 30 consecutive or accumulative days in any 36-month period. The maximum amount payable will be equal to 2/3 of the initial permanent duty CCA, less any amount paid within the past 36 months for temporary duty under paragraph 8–4c(1).

8–5. Procedures for requesting allowances

a. Officers and enlisted Soldiers who must wear civilian clothing full time in performing official duties and who are eligible for a CCA will request it no later than 30 days prior to departure or upon arrival at the new duty assignment or TDY station. However, officers and enlisted Soldiers who are eligible to receive a CCA, and who are reporting on a permanent change of station to an OCONUS location, may receive payment 90 days prior to their report date as stated on their orders to eliminate undue hardship on the Soldier because of the unavailability and cost of clothing at OCONUS locations.

(1) Although an individual may be paid up to 3 months (90 days) in advance, this will in no way affect the Soldier's "anniversary" date for subsequent payment at the end of the tour. The request for a CCA will be submitted in memorandum format, one Soldier per request, directly from the Soldier's unit commander to the approving ACOM and will include all the information necessary as it pertains to the officer or the enlisted Soldier. Failure to furnish the following will cause delays in processing and possible disapproval: Name, rank, SSN, MOS, and special skill identifier.

(2) A written justification is extremely important in deciding the approval for CCA. If the request for a CCA is submitted because the TDY or assignment orders indicate civilian clothing is required, a copy of the orders must be included. If the orders do not state a requirement for civilian clothing but the request for a CCA is submitted because of the host Government's requirement based upon the DOD Foreign Clearance Guide or direction of the ACOM commander or the U. S. Ambassador, then the request must include this information, as well as a copy of the directive. If the request for a CCA is submitted because the Soldier is required to wear civilian clothing full time for official duty for reasons other than host the Government, then a written justification must be included. This justification must be detailed enough so that the request can stand alone and describe details as it pertains to intelligence, security, or related activities. The justification must include the following:

(a) The date of expiration term of service, retirement, or release from active duty.

(b) The date the Soldier physically arrived at their current assignment.

(c) The date the Soldier is due to physically rotate from the assignment; the date eligible for return from OCONUS or permanent change of station date.

(d) The new date of departure from the assignment due to an extension.

(e) The start and end dates of the CCA assignment.

(f) The mandatory wear date of civilian clothing.

Note. This date must be inclusive in paragraph 8–5b.

b. The request will include the following statement, which would be verified by the commander: "This Soldier will be required to wear civilian clothing full time for official duty for approximately (number) months."

8–6. Procedures for receiving clothing allowance

a. A memorandum from the ACOM approving authority authorizing payment of CCA will be sent to the local Defense Military Pay Office. A courtesy copy of the approval memorandum will be returned to the Soldier's unit for their personnel file.

b. Commanders have direct supervision and responsibility for expenditures. They will ensure that—

(1) Full use is made of garments provided under the clothing allowance system.

(2) Only clothing items required in performing duties are purchased.

(3) The Soldier must purchase clothing within 30 days of receipt of the allowance. Purchase will be verified by presenting the sales receipt(s) to the Soldier's supervisor or unit commander.

(4) Payment of allowances is to be recorded in the Soldier's pay and allowances record.

(5) If a Soldier does not use the funds for the purpose authorized, the unit commander, together with the local DFAS, will prepare a DD Form 139 start collection action against the Soldier.

(6) If a Soldier does not receive the funds because of a change in assignment or release from active duty, the unit commander will endorse the original memorandum back to the approving ACOM approving authority for accountability purposes.

(7) Civilian clothing items issued or purchased under this regulation are expendable property. They are dropped from military accountability. A Soldier may permanently retain civilian garments issued to them. However, the civilian garments must be available for use in other assignments within the 3 years from the date of the approved authorization.

(8) Officer and enlisted Soldiers who must wear civilian clothing are responsible for the upkeep of their military clothing during the time they wear civilian clothing.

Chapter 9
Supply of Individual Clothing for Senior and Junior Reserve Officers' Training Corps

9–1. Purchase limitations

a. Uniform items, including footwear, clothing, and embellishments such as insignia and devices, may be provided to educational institutions hosting ROTC programs. Acquisition is limited to those items authorized in CTA 50–900. ROTC units will submit requisitions using DA Form 2765–1 (Request for Issue Or Turn-In) to the proper support installation, or as otherwise prescribed by HQ, U.S. Army Cadet Command (USACC). Emergency requirements for ROTC units may be submitted to AMCS per paragraph 9–5e.

b. Purchases from AMCS are limited to those items in paragraph 9–1a. Individual ROTC cadets are not authorized to purchase items except as provided in paragraph 3–1k. When the installation commander determines the AMCS is unable to provide clothing, the institutions will submit requisitions using DA Form 2765–1 to the correct supply source.

c. An institution may want ROTC military science (MS) IV cadets, scheduled to be commissioned, to wear the prescribed Army uniform at graduation or commissioning exercises. The institution may, prior to 90 days of anticipated date of commissioning, act as the agent for the cadet and purchase the uniforms or clothing for the cadets on a cash basis only. An ROTC cadet is not authorized a uniform allowance until they have been commissioned, reported for active duty, and passed a physical examination. A cadet, therefore, will not purchase a uniform for commissioning, nor will the student be asked to reimburse institutional funds. Purchases under this authority—

(1) May be made from AMCS.

(2) Are limited to within 90 days before graduation.

d. On receipt of a certificate of pregnancy, the PMS may authorize the purchase of maternity ASU and maternity ACU for SROTC cadets per CTA 50–900. For RPA and OMA, funds will be used as appropriated. Use closest AMCS or online military catalog sales procedures to purchase ASUs. Use standard Army supply procedures to procure the ACU, except when a catalog or credit card purchase is authorized because of remote location of the ROTC unit. Purchases are limited to one ASU and one ACU per pregnant SROTC cadet. Inventory of maternity uniforms at unit level is not authorized.

9–2. Limitations of issue

a. Uniforms and equipment are issued only to enrolled members of the ROTC program. The use of uniforms and equipment is limited to activities that best achieve Army objectives.

b. Foreign students who meet criteria established in AR 145–1 are authorized uniforms to wear.

c. Conditional and auditing students are not authorized Government-purchased uniforms and equipment or commutation allowance (see AR 145–1).

9–3. Conservation of uniform clothing

a. The PMS or senior Army instructor at each ROTC unit ensures that serviceable uniforms on hand are applied against current and future needs based on firm enrollment data.

b. Cleaning and restoring issue-in-kind uniforms and making authorized alterations (such as sleeve and trouser lengths, minor changes in waist measurements, and sewing on authorized embellishments) are done before the issue or reissue to ROTC cadets. This is done under contract at the lowest rates, consistent with satisfactory workmanship. Cost is at Government expense, except as indicated in paragraphs 9–3b(1) and 9–3b(2).

(1) Purchases, restoring of uniforms, and footwear will be funded using appropriated funds.

(2) The student pays for cleaning and normal maintenance of uniforms and footwear in their possession. The student is not required to clean the uniform for turn in. Also, the student is not required to pay for costs of repair and restoration caused by FWT.

c. Under the allowances prescribed in CTA 50–900, each enrolled ROTC cadet is authorized one pair of shoes. Male and female cadets are also authorized two pairs of cotton socks.

(1) Maintenance, repair, and replacement of shoes, combat boots, and socks, while in the possession of the cadet, are at the expense of the cadet, except under conditions in paragraph 9–3c(2).

(2) At educational institutions, where uniforms are furnished on an issue-in-kind basis, replacement of shoes, combat boots, and socks lost or destroyed while in the possession of the cadet is at the expense of the Government only when the loss or destruction was not the fault of or due to neglect of the cadet and occurred during ROTC training.

9–4. Requisitioning channels

a. Supply of individual clothing and distinctive insignia normally comes from distribution depots. Supply from support installations may be made as provided in paragraph 9–4c, under the following conditions:

(1) When stock is available to meet ROTC requirements and an overall savings to the Government is realized. Support installation requisitioning objectives will not be increased to meet annual ROTC requirements.

(2) When the educational institution is located near support installation, the use of Government vehicles is authorized when available at the installation.

b. All requisitions, including those for special measurement items, are submitted to the supply source through the support installation, unless otherwise prescribed by HQ, USACC. The support installation provides the fund cite and sends the requisition to the proper supply source. The supply source sends the shipment directly to the ROTC unit.

c. Excess serviceable stocks of ROTC clothing will be turned in to the supporting installation supply division.

9–5. Requisitioning procedures

a. For requisitions placed on DLA activities or National Inventory Control Points (see AR 725–50).

b. DA Form 2765–1, as prescribed by HQ, USACC, is used to request items of clothing. Assign and record a document number from the expendable/durable document register for ROTC unit's clothing requests.

c. ROTC units submit requisitions using DA Form 2765–1 for uniform items for the following year after the close of the current school year. ROTC funds are cited on all requisitions. Requisitions are prepared as follows:

(1) Requisitions normally are based on the actual enrollment at the beginning of the previous school year, less quantities of serviceable items on hand. Quantities may be increased to provide likely increases in enrollment. Caution must be taken in the quantities approved to prevent excesses at ROTC unit.

(2) Maximum inventory is authorized for emergency, replacement, and sizing. The ROTC units may retain an amount not to exceed 20 percent of enrollment for sized uniform requirements.

(3) Additional uniforms may be requisitioned at later enrollment periods if stocks on hand are insufficient or cannot be used to fill the requirement. In these cases, the requisition is based on the actual measurements (nearest tariff size) of the cadets who cannot be furnished uniforms from present stocks. Requisitions of this nature will be held to the minimum.

d. For JROTC cadets, an amount not to exceed an excess of 20 percent of sized uniformed items based on JROTC enrollment may be requisitioned and stocked at all JROTC units for emergency replacement, sizing, and distribution.

e. To accommodate emergency requirements for ROTC units, the following procedures apply:

(1) When ROTC units determine that an emergency exists for items of clothing that normal requisitioning time frames will not accommodate, a DA Form 3078 for each cadet will be prepared to acquire items from the AMCS at the support installation. Unit supply sergeant or specialist will submit the DA Form 3078 in accordance with paragraph 1–6*p*.

(2) The procedures for submitting the hard copy DA Form 3078 are listed below. Regardless of method, appropriate completion of the form as well as documentation is still required. For a hard copy submission, the following procedures will apply:

(a) Bulk issues of clothing will not be processed. The DA Form 3078 will be prepared in seven copies, with one copy retained for the unit's suspense file and the remaining six copies forwarded to the support installation budget analyst controlling funds for the ROTC unit's support.

(b) The budget analyst will provide certification of fund availability and place applicable cost code data on the DA Form 3078 in block 30. One copy is retained by the analyst for fund control, and the remaining five copies are forwarded to the AMCS.

(c) The AMCS will complete the transaction and return one copy to the individual or unit, retain two copies for AMCS use, and forward the remaining two copies, batched under ROTC, to the servicing installation. In the event the item is not available, the document will be returned through the support installation budget analyst to the institution.

f. The above procedures apply only to emergency requirements for ROTC units and are not intended to cover routine supply transactions. ROTC units will verify availability of items prior to submission to the AMCS. Items not available from AMCS will be requested through the installation supply division budget analyst.

9–6. Measuring instructions

a. Nonrecoverable items. HQ, USACC establishes and implements procedures for the management and control of nonrecoverable items.

b. Uniform items. Taking measurements of ROTC cadets to requisition sized uniform items is governed by the applicable fitting manuals.

c. Special sizes. ROTC cadets of unusual stature require clothing in sizes other than those listed in the size schedules.

(1) Instructions for measuring these cadets are on DD Form 358 and DD Form 1111.

(2) These forms are attached to requisitions for special size clothing items. Requisitions are sent to the Commander, DLA–TS (DLA–TS–FRC) (Room 310), 700 Robbins Avenue, Philadelphia, PA 19111–5092.

d. Shoe measurement. Applicable fitting manuals contain instructions for measuring shoes requisitioned from Government sources. Procedures for supply of special measurement footwear are contained in chapter 7. A DD Form 150 is completed for a student requiring special footwear. The form is attached to special measurement shoe requisitions. The requisitions are mailed to the Veterans Integrated Service Network, 3 Department of Veterans Affairs Medical Center (Network Prosthetics), 423 East 23rd Street, New York, NY 10010–5011.

9–7. Supply of individual clothing through commutation of uniform allowance
See chapter 10.

9–8. Purchase of individual clothing items from Army stocks
See paragraph 9–1.

9–9. Issue and sale of footwear and purchase of personal clothing items

a. Accountability for combat boots, low quarter shoes, women's pumps, and nonrecoverable items will not be maintained by the military property custodian (MPC), military property specialist (MPS), Army ROTC property book officer (PBO) or primary hand-receipt holder after issue to Army ROTC cadets. Issues to cadets will be recorded on hand receipts.

b. Army ROTC cadets will be responsible for leather footwear issued to them. SROTC cadets who fail to complete the first school year of both the basic or advanced course, and JROTC cadets who fail to complete the first year of the program will be given an opportunity to purchase leather footwear at 50 percent of the current sales price. Cadets not desiring to retain the shoes or boots on this basis will turn them in with all other clothing items. Disposition of items turned in will be as prescribed by HQ, USACC under proper accountability exemption provision per AR 710–2. Reimbursement or turn-in by ROTC cadets will not be required for such items that have been in their possession for one or more complete school years. Accountability will be reestablished for leather footwear by preparing DA Form 4949 (Administrative Adjustment Report (AAR)) as "Cadet Return," with an attached roster of students (see DA Pam 710–2–1). The administrative adjustment report will be recorded on the document register and posted to the property book. Used boots and shoes will be posted to a separate property book page with the word "Unserviceable" printed on the first and last transaction lines to allow accounting for used and new footwear. Bulk turn-in of unserviceable items will be conducted at least annually. Turn-in will be made to the supporting installation. Reimbursement or turn-in will not be required for such items that have been in the possession of the student for one or more complete school years.

c. CTA 50–900 prescribes the ROTC authorized allowances for issue of personal clothing to each SROTC cadet. SROTC cadets may purchase the ROTC authorized allowance of personal clothing items, less shoes, and recoverable items that have been used for 2 school years (also applicable to clothing issued as replacement due to FWT and for newly fielded clothing items issued) at 50 percent of the current sales price contained in DOD EMALL. This provision also exists for cadets who are to be commissioned through the early commissioning program or those who have completed MS IV within 90 days of expected commissioning.

d. Collection and accounting procedures for footwear and uniform sales to ROTC cadets are as follows:

(1) At educational institutions where the Army has property accountability, payment will be made by postal or bank money order, cashier's or certified checks drawn payable to the DFAS and name of the supporting installation. This precludes the need to handle coins and currency. The Army ROTC PBO or primary hand-receipt holder officer will transmit pay instruments to the DFAS of the applicable support installation with a completed DD Form 362 (Statement of Charges/Cash Collection Voucher) made in triplicate. The collection voucher will show that the amounts remitted represent payment for the applicable quantity and type items purchased. The ROTC unit representative will file a receipted copy from the DFAS.

(2) Educational institutions with property accountability will prescribe procedures for collecting from individual cadets. Such institutions will prepare and forward its check or money order for total sales to the DFAS of the support educational installation. The institution remittance will be accompanied by a statement, which clearly shows the quantity and type of items sold to cadets. The total price will equal the remittance check or money order.

(3) The DFAS of the support installation will prepare the DD Form 362 for all remittances received from institutions. The DFAS will return a receipted copy, along with the original, as the institution's statement reflecting quantities and types of items for filing as a credit voucher. If payment instruments are made payable to the U.S. Treasury, these will be accepted and processed immediately notwithstanding the inscription.

(4) Collections will be credited as "appropriation refunds" identified to the specific fiscal station of the applicable support installation.

9–10. Accounting for clothing

a. All individual clothing items, including insignia, are exempt from formal property accountability procedures contained in AR 710–2. HQ, USACC is responsible for developing measures to control and safeguard clothing items against fraud, waste and abuse.

b. Individual clothing items will be issued to cadets on DA Form 3645–1. The individual receiving the property will sign and date the clothing record acknowledging property responsibility in the event of loss or damage to property (see AR 735–5).

c. In cases where one PBO, MPC, or MPS is accountable for multiple ROTC units (several high schools with JROTC or extension centers or cross enrolled schools with SROTC), separate jacket files will be maintained for receipts covering clothing items issued to each. The PBO, MPC, or MPS may issue clothing items in bulk to each activity on DA Form 2062 (Hand Receipt/Annex Number). Issues to individual cadets will then be done by the hand receipt holder as specified in paragraphs 9–11a through 9–11e. In this instance, the hand receipt holder maintains the student clothing hand receipts on file at the ROTC unit.

d. All JROTC and SROTC cadets are required sign a statement declaring, "I understand that, if I owe a debt to the Government related to the loss, damaged or destruction of individual clothing, I consent to the notification of the debt to my parent or guardian and notification of the debt, together with a request to my education institution that my grades and transcript be withheld pending payment of the debt."

9–11. Storage of clothing at the end of the school year

a. At the end of the school year, all clothing issued to ROTC cadets will be turned in to the PBO, MPC, or MPS or designated hand receipt holder.

b. The PMS may authorize enrolled SROTC cadets to retain non-recoverable items during the summer months. Also, the PMS may authorize cadets scheduled to attend SROTC advanced camp or ranger camp to retain additional items.

c. The MPC of JROTC units may authorize enrolled JROTC cadets to retain nonrecoverable items only.

d. Enrolled ROTC cadets (senior or junior) are not required to have clothing items cleaned prior to turn-in.

e. The PBO or MPC (SROTC or JROTC units) will have clothing cleaned and renovated in accordance with existing instructions. Storage will be in such a manner as to simplify reissue to ROTC cadets the following school year.

9–12. Financial liability investigation of property

Lost, damaged, or destroyed individual clothing items by cadets will be accounted for in accordance with AR 735–5 (not applicable to footwear).

a. If a ROTC cadet admits negligence, allow the cadet to reimburse the Government using Statement of Charges/ Cash Collection Voucher collection procedures. Cadet payments will be processed as prescribed by the educational institution.

b. On a quarterly basis, the educational institution will forward to the support installation DFAS a check or U.S. postal money order made payable to the DFAS. The reimbursement will be accompanied by a completed DD Form 362 in triplicate. The DFAS of the support installation will review DD Form 362 for adequacy and deposit the funds. A receipted copy of the DD Form 362 will be returned to the institution's ROTC unit for use, as applicable.

c. If the ROTC cadet does not admit liability or drops out of the ROTC program without returning individual clothing items, initiate a DD Form 200 (Financial Liability Investigation of Property Loss) in accordance with AR 735–5.

d. If, after following all the procedures set out in AR 735–5, the approval authority determines that financial liability is appropriate, efforts to recoup the debt to the Government will be made, to include the following:

(1) A letter to parent or guardian sent certified mail, return receipt requested, notifying them of debt.

(2) A letter to the educational institution requesting grades and transcripts will be withheld pending collection of the debt.

e. The initiator will ensure DD Form 200, block 1 and blocks 3 through 11 are completed. Block 13 will be left blank. The DD Form 200 will be assigned a document number and signed by the accountable officer prior to forwarding the DD Form 200 to the approving authority. The appointing and approving authority will complete blocks 13 and 14 as applicable and in accordance with AR 735–5. In no case will an approving authority relieve a cadet when there is evidence, prima facie or otherwise, of negligence.

Chapter 10
Commutation of Uniforms for Reserve Officers' Training Corps Activities

10–1. Introduction

Commutation is monetary payment the Government makes to enrolled MSI and II and contracted MS III Senior ROTC cadets instead of providing issue-in-kind uniforms. See table 10–1, which lists institutions qualifying and approved for commutation as civilian college with corps of cadets.

Table 10–1
Institutions qualifying and approved for commutation

Type	Names
Military colleges	Virginia Military Institute Norwich University The Citadel North Georgia College
Military Junior Colleges	Valley Forge Military Academy and Junior College Georgia Military College Wentworth Military School and Junior College Marion Institute New Mexico Military Institute

Table 10–1
Institutions qualifying and approved for commutation—Continued

Civilian colleges with a corps of cadets	Virginia Polytechnic Institute and State University Texas A&M, College Station Mary Baldwin College and/or Virginia Women Institute for Leadership

10–2. Requesting commutation funds
The authorized representative of the educational institution electing commutation of uniforms or reverting to issue-in-kind uniforms must request authority by 1 June of the year proceeding the preferred effective school year. The request will show the total probable number of students in MS I, MS II, MS III, and MS IV. Requests will be forwarded to the Commander, USACC (ATCC–TT), Fort Knox, KY 40121–5205.

10–3. Restrictions on payments
Institutions identified in table 10–1 will draw issue-in-kind uniforms for cadets enrolled in a partnership school.

10–4. Payments of funds
Commutation payments will be made directly to the cadet after initial probationary period of enrollment, not to exceed 60 days.

10–5. Authorized activities
Commutation funds will be expended to support only the following activities:

  a. Uniform items, issue-in-kind, or issue to cadets on campus.

  b. Uniform items, cadet-type, worn similar to issue-in-kind uniform items. This includes traditional uniform items, such as capes, when worn with the cadet-type uniform and insignia and accessories (see AR 145–1).

10–6. Disposing of uniforms
Uniforms bought with commutation funds are not Government property and do not require accountability as prescribed in AR 710–2 and DA Pam 710–2–1. Uniforms bought with commutation funds become the personal property of the cadet.

10–7. Uniform commutation rates
Commutation rates are provided annually by the OSD. This rate is to cover the cost of cadet uniform purchases. However, cadets may be required to pay out of pocket any cost in excess of the amount of commutation payments received from the Government to purchase uniforms. Personnel includes the following:

  a. Basic course members of MS I and MS II enrolled at qualifying schools identified in table 10–1. Definition of enrolled basic course cadet is contained in AR 145–1. A payment is provided to cadets for the MS I and MS II school years. The MS I and MS II school year last 9 months each. Cadets may be required by the school to pay any costs in excess of the amount the cadet receives from the Government to purchase uniforms.

  b. Contracted advanced course members of MS III and MS IV, enrolled at qualifying schools identified in table 10–1. A one-time payment to the cadet to cover uniform expenses for the MS III and MS IV school years (18 months) is made at the beginning of the MS III year. Cadets may be required by the school to pay any costs in excess of the amount the cadet receives from the Government to purchase uniforms. However, if a cadet contracts during the MS IV year, only one-half of the established MS III rate will be paid.

  c. Students not eligible for commutation funds—

  (1) Generally, those that are not fully enrolled (see AR 145–1).

  (2) Auditing students as described in AR 145–1.

  (3) Conditional students per AR 145–1. However, when conditional status is changed to enrolled, cadet is authorized commutation payment (see AR 145–1).

  (4) Foreign student not meeting criteria established in AR 145–1.

10–8. Functions
  a. During December of each year, the Director, DLA–TS will provide the military department the current price list of uniform items to be used the following fiscal year.

  b. DFAS will—

  (1) Process cadet commutation payments via the DJMS–Reserve Component (RC) or ROTC for those submitted by the battalion that are certified-eligible to receive commutation.

  (2) Provide commutation obligation feedback to USACC via the DJMS–RC or ROTC pay system monthly output report reflecting commutation payments by cadet, by school. The monthly pay reports reflect the payment by cadet, which are sent to the host ROTC battalion.

c. The DCS, G–1 will—

(1) Prescribe the standard uniform items (for basic and advanced Cadets) in quantities authorized to be provided.

(2) Develop the commutation rates, based on the standard military Army service uniform and established procedures for rate reviews on an annual basis.

(3) Submit to the ASA (ALT) an estimate of the rates of commutation based on the latest DLA–TS clothing rate, by sex and course, not later than 1 July of each year.

(4) Classify educational institutions as military colleges or military junior colleges.

d. The Commander, U.S. Army Accessions Command will develop responsibility to—

(1) Budget for commutation funds.

(2) Provide funds to DFAS.

(3) Submit pay transaction via the DJMS–RC or ROTC pay system for issuance of payment to those cadets determined eligible by the ROTC battalion for uniform commutation allowance. These payments will be made via the electronic funds transfer to the checking or savings account on file with the DJMS–RC or ROTC pay systems. Those cadets without a checking or savings account will receive a hardcopy check made payable to the cadet at the host ROTC battalion address.

(4) Establish policies and procedures to ensure that requisitions of authorized CTA 50–900, do not result in inventory excess beyond those authorized by this regulation.

(5) Prescribe policies and procedures for the procurement, issue, and wear of cadet insignia, awards, badges, and decorations that are not in contravention with existing law or policy.

(6) Assist the DCS, G–1 with the estimation of annual commutation rates.

e. The ROTC Brigade Headquarters will—

(1) Provide assistance to institutions requesting to change from commutation funds to the issue-in-kind system and vice versa. Final approval must be obtained from the CG, USACC.

(2) Ensure cadet information is accurately entered into the cadet command database.

(3) During regularly scheduled inspections, validate school's eligibility to participate in commutation.

f. The PMS will—

(1) Prepare and pre-certify all pay transactions for uniform commutation for all eligible cadets via the cadet database.

(2) Ensure cadet eligibility to commutation payment.

(3) Commutation payment is included in the end-of-month check that may also include monthly subsistence and flat rate book payment, depending on the status of the cadet. The PMS must verify amounts for accuracy prior to transmission of the data to HQ, USACC.

(4) If an underpayment or overpayment is identified, the administrative technician will immediately contact their respective pay point of contact at HQ, USACC, Pay Operations Division for assistance. Ensure return of any hardcopy unclaimed checks to HQ, USACC, Pay Operations Division, Fort Knox, KY 40121–5205

(5) Process within 10 days of receipt.

10–9. Eligibility for uniform commutation funds

Commutation is payable to ROTC members enrolled in the basic (MS I and MS II) and advanced courses (MS III and MS IV) for at least 45 consecutive days under the following conditions:

a. Basic course. The current rate of commutation funds is payable for each enrolled member 45 days after entry into MS I and MS II. A member compressing MS I and MS II will be authorized payment of commutation funds only once during the school year.

b. Advanced course. The rate of commutation funds in effect during the school year that the claim is made is payable only once for each contracted member. This is 45 days after enrollment in the advanced course and normally occurs at the MS III level. The rate is paid at the MSIII and MS IV years, and no further payments are authorized. However, if a cadet contracts in the MS IV year, then the rate of payment will be made at half the rate of that of the MS III rate.

c. Conditional students. These are not payable for participating conditional students or noncontracted advanced course cadets; however, commutation may be paid to conditional students who become eligible and have enrolled for at least 45 days.

10–10. How to obtain uniform commutation funds

Guidance for proper documentation for commutation payments is included in the cadet database, Battalion End Users Manual, and the DJMS–RC or ROTC Procedural Guidance Manual for School Year Operations.

10–11. Inactivation or change in system

Guidance for proper documentation for commutation payments is included in the Cadet Command Information Management System database, Battalion End Users Manual and the DJMS–RC or ROTC Procedural Guidance Manual for School Year Operations. (User must have special permission to access site from U.S. Army Accessions Command, Deputy Director Information Support Activity CIO/G–6.)

10–12. Transfer of basic and advanced course enrolled members

a. Basic course cadets may not claim commutation for a MS school year if the cadet had received commutation payment while attending another school as listed at table 10–1.

b. Advanced course cadets may not claim commutation funds if commutation funds were paid to the cadet for participation in advanced course while attending another school as listed at table 10–1.

c. With the approval of the PMS at the gaining military school, an additional commutation is authorized for cadets who have been transferred because of discontinuance of the program at a previous school.

Chapter 11
Transfer of Enlisted Soldiers on Active Duty

11–1. Losing command

a. Upon receipt of a Soldier's assignment orders, the unit commander directs a clothing inspection or inventory for each Soldier; however, commanders may permit corporals through sergeants major to furnish a statement, as shown in table 1–1, that they have all their clothing and items are serviceable. For Soldiers with 6 months (180 days) or more of active service, a copy of DA Form 3078 will be retained until all initial issues have been completed and the Soldier has reached their initial permanent duty station. Items of clothing in Soldiers' possession are inventoried against their personal clothing allowances. Each item is inspected for serviceability, fit, and appearance. Soldiers being reassigned for separation must sign a receipt or a turn-in (see para 12–10). Shortages are made up by cash purchases.

b. Initial and supplemental allowance items that are unserviceable or are not in the possession of the Soldier are repaired or replaced at the Soldier's expense. Supplemental allowance items need not be maintained after duty is completed (see exception in para 4–6b).

c. Enlisted Soldiers normally transfer with a complete initial allowance of clothing items. When a clothing item is not available to complete initial allowances, the enlisted Soldier is transferred without complete allowances.

d. A copy of DA Form 3078 is retained with the Soldier's unit file until all initial issues have been completed and the Soldier reaches their initial permanent duty station.

e. Excluded are enlisted Soldiers leaving an OCONUS area to continental United States (CONUS) for immediate separation. Clothing shortages and replacements are obtained at the Soldier's expense.

f. For transfer of OCIE items, see paragraphs 6–5b(1) and 6–5b(2).

11–2. Gaining command

a. On arrival of Soldiers reassigned to an activity for permanent duty, the unit commander directs a clothing inspection or inventory for enlisted personnel. However, commanders may permit corporals through sergeants major to furnish a statement, as shown in table 1–1, that they have all their clothing and that items are serviceable.

b. Shortages of previously issued items, disclosed by inspections or inventories, are replaced at the Soldier's expense. Unserviceable items are repaired or replaced at the Soldier's expense.

c. Shortages in initial allowances must be obtained within 15 days after assignment.

d. Upon completion of initial issues of transferrable OCIE, commanders will transpose completed issues of transferrable OCIE to DA Form 3645 in accordance with paragraph 6-5b(2) and AR 710–2.

11–3. Clearance from clothing repair, Army military clothing stores, and alteration facilities

a. When an enlisted Soldier is transferred to another station, the unit commander has the enlisted Soldier obtain clearance from the AMCS installation clothing repair and alteration facilities before leaving the station. This does not apply on transfer to a hospital as a patient. The facility completes a DA Form 137–2 (Installation Clearance Record), in duplicate for each Soldier. Instructions are printed on the form.

b. Unit commanders advise enlisted Soldiers alerted for movement or placed on orders that they are responsible for clothing and footwear left in commercial establishments or the Exchange.

c. When an enlisted Soldier is transferred to a hospital as a patient, the unit commander is responsible for getting the clearance. If articles of personal clothing or footwear left for repair or alteration in either Government or civilian facilities are not ready at the time the enlisted Soldier transfers, arrangements will be made to ship the items to the Soldier at the new station. These shipments are made at Government expense.

Chapter 12
Retention and Disposition of Clothing

12–1. Introduction

a. Enlisted Soldiers will retain all non-recoverable items when discharged or separated from active or reserve duty service. ARNG Soldiers will retain personal clothing per appendix C of the ARNG CCD User Handbook. Enlisted Soldiers being transferred to a USAR Control Group will retain personal clothing per table 12–1.

Table 12–1
Retention of personal clothing items for Soldiers transferred to U.S. Army Reserve control groups

Transferred From	Type of Transfer	MOS qualified	6 mos or less service	Clothing retained 6 mos, and 3 yrs	Clothing retained 4 years	DA Form 4886 required	Responsible for completion of DA Form 4886	Other requirements
Active Army	Normal release from active duty (REFRAD) at expiration term of service AR 635–200	Yes	All[1]	All	All	Yes	CDR of last unit of assignment or attachment?	Member signs the statement as shown in figure 12–5.
	Completion of IADT (IRR Direct enlistment) AR 601–210	No	N/A	N/A	N/A	N/A	N/A	N/A
ARNG USAR Unit	Completion of required service AR 135–91	Yes	All[2]	All[2]	All[2]	Yes	Same as #1	Same as #1
	Unsatisfactory unit participation AR 135–91	No	N/A	N/A	N/A	No	N/A	None
	Released to active duty	N/A	N/A	N/A	N/A			
Active Army, ARNG or USAR unit	Did not meet medical procurement standards, sole surviving son or daughter or parenthood AR 635–200 and AR 135–178							
	Dependency/Hardship/Parenthood AR 635–200 and AR 135–178	Yes	All[2,3]	All[2,3]	All[2,3]	Yes	Same as #1	Same as #1
	Pregnancy AR 635–200 and AR 135–178							
	AR 135–178							
	Entry level performance AR 635–200 and AR 135–178	No	None[4]	None[4]	N/A	No	N/A	None
	Unsatisfactory Performance AR 635–200 and AR 135–178							

Notes:
1. IRR direct enlistees will have their clothing adjusted to full allowances prior to transfer to IRR.
2. ARNG Soldiers will retain clothing as determined by the appropriate State Adjutant General.
3. Retention of uniforms includes only those items already issued to the Soldier prior to identification for reissue. No further adjustments are authorized.
4. Nonrecoverable items, such as underwear and footwear, may be retained by the Soldier.
5. This includes those Soldiers who immediately reenlist in the IRR or discharge from the Active Army.

b. Personal clothing allowances will not be brought up to date when a person is discharged or separated from the Service. This includes enlisted Soldiers leaving an OCONUS area for CONUS for immediate separation.

c. When personnel do not have the items that are normally turned in, processing will be as follows:

(1) Enlisted Soldiers will reimburse the Government for missing recoverable type clothing.

(2) Enlisted Soldiers are not required to pay for items never received or can provide proof items were previously turned in.

d. Items are turned in at last duty station.

(1) *U.S. Army Reserve and Active duty personnel.* At time of turn-in, a DA Form 3078 is prepared, in triplicate, and properly annotated. The receiving facility retains the original copy. The individual retains a copy. One copy is placed in the enlisted Soldier's Interactive Personnel Electronic Records Management System (IPERMS)).

(2) *Army National Guard personnel.* At time of turn-in, a CCDF Form 3161 (Request for Turn-In) or CCDF Form 3161M (Request for Turn-In Manual) is prepared and properly annotated, to include commissioned officer certification of the FWT status of unserviceable items. Two copies, in addition to any required to physically accompany the turn-in, are produced. The individual retains one copy, and one copy is placed in the enlisted Soldier's IPERMS.

e. Personnel transferring to ARNG or USAR will, in every instance, report to their unit with all personal clothing items. DA Form 4886 will be used to establish accountability.

f. Personnel transferring to USAR control groups will retain personal clothing per table 12–1.

12–2. Personnel with more than 3 years active duty

a. Active Army personnel with more than 3 years active duty who are discharged under honorable conditions may retain all clothing items in their possession. Turn-in of recoverable items is determined by the unit commander.

b. Personnel who are Release From Active Duty (REFRAD) and transferred to ARNG or USAR units will, in every instance, retain all personal clothing in their possession. Voluntary turn-in of these items is not authorized. DA Form 4886 will be used to establish accountability. See paragraph 12–10 and table 12–2 and the RC personnel update.

c. Active Army personnel who are REFRAD and transferred to USAR control groups will retain personal clothing per table 12–1. (See the RC personnel update).

12–3. Personnel with 3 years or fewer active duty

a. Active Army personnel who are discharged under honorable conditions with 3 years or less active duty are permitted to retain all clothing items.

b. Active Army personnel who are REFRAD and transferred to ARNG or USAR units will, in every instance, retain all clothing items in their possession. DA Form 4886 will be used to establish accountability (see table 12–2 para 12–10).

c. Active Army personnel who are REFRAD and transferred to USAR control groups will retain personal clothing per table 12–1. (See the RC personnel update).

12–4. Personnel with 6 months (180 days) or less active duty service

a. Personnel with 6 months (180 days) or less active duty service who received an honorable, general, or other than honorable discharge may retain one ASU and component items. Soldiers who are processed under deferred issue procedures and who are separated or discharged before they receive a complete issue will not receive further issue, to include the ASU. Processing persons discharged or separated from service for medical reasons discussed in paragraph 12–7.

b. Personnel with fewer than 6 months (180 days) of duty who are REFRAD and transferred to USAR control groups will retain personal clothing per table 12–1.

12–5. Soldiers of the Reserve Components on initial active duty for training

a. When training is completed, the RC Soldier will return to home station with all personal clothing issued at the Army training center. Those items that are in need of repair or exchange will be repaired or exchanged by the training installation. Accountability will be established by DA Form 4886, which will be completed by the training unit commander prior to the Soldier's departure from training. The original is to be filed in the Soldier's IPERMS. Personal clothing issued in excess of the RC allowances is kept by the Soldier on return to home station. When this occurs, replacement under the issue-in-kind system is not made until USAR allowances specified in CTA 50–900 are reached.

b. All OCIE items are turned in unless the local installation commander directs otherwise.

c. When ARNG trainees fail to complete training and are released back to their home stations, their clothing issue will be withdrawn. The following procedures apply:

(1) The training unit commander, or the designee, inventories each trainee's personal clothing, documenting the inventory on a DA Form 3078 by entering the unit, home station designation, and quantities of items inventoried.

(2) One copy of DA Form 3078 will be placed in a trainee's IPERMS for return to the trainee's ARNG unit and one copy is mailed to the trainee's State USPFO.

(3) Training unit will turn-in recovered personal clothing, using CCDF Form 3078, CCDF Form 3161, or CCDF Form 3161M and copies of the member's orders to the installation clothing recovery facility.

(4) Upon receipt by the installation clothing recovery facility, the clothing and DA Form 3078 will be inventoried. The installation will ensure that credit is provided to the NGB based on the ratio of turn-ins that were ARNG compared with the total of Active Army, USAR, and ARNG. Credit provided will be 50 percent of the DOD EMALL price for Condition Code B recovered items.

(5) The installation clothing recovery facility will retain one copy and send the second copy of DA Form 3078 to the supporting DFAS for forwarding to the Soldier's home station USPFO.

d. Clothing of ARNG trainees dropped from the rolls or discharged at training installations will be withdrawn. The procedures indicated in paragraphs 12–5c(1) through 12–5c(5) apply.

e. When a USAR trainee fails to complete training, they turn-in all clothing and equipment. Nonrecoverable items are excluded. The following procedures apply:

(1) Procedures discussed in paragraph 12–5c(1) apply to the training unit commander.

(2) The installation supply officer will—

(a) Classify items.

(b) Determine serviceability.

(c) Credit RPA funds.

(d) Transfer used serviceable items to the AMCS if required for sale or issue.

(e) Turn in unserviceable items to the DRMS.

12–6. Soldiers of the Reserve Components who transfer from Reserve Components to Active Army

Enlisted Soldiers who are being discharged to join the Active Army will retain 100 percent of their personal clothing. A 100 percent inventory will be conducted prior to release. All shortages will be accounted for under AR 735–5. All totals will be brought forward to the next blank column of the DA Form 4886. The original DA Form 4886 will be forwarded to the Soldier's gaining unit. One copy will be hand carried by the Soldier to the gaining unit. A copy will be maintained at unit level for 90 days.

12–7. Personnel being discharged or separated for medical reasons

a. Personnel who are honorably discharged or separated for medical reasons and who have completed 6 months (180 days) or more active duty may retain personal clothing items.

b. Personnel discharged or separated before they complete 6 months (180 days) of active duty may retain one Army Service Uniform, component items, and nonrecoverable items that were issued prior to individual being identified for separation or discharge.

c. Civilian outer clothing will be issued, if necessary. The cost to the Government will not exceed $40 for each individual.

d. Personnel REFRAD and transferred to USAR control groups will retain personal clothing items that were issued prior to being identified for discharge per table 12–1.

12–8. Personnel accepting a commission or warrant officer appointment

Personnel discharged to accept a commission or appointment as a warrant officer may retain all authorized items of personal clothing in their possession at the time of appointment. This includes ARNG and USAR personnel.

12–9. Personnel discharged under bad conduct or dishonorable conditions

a. Soldiers who receive a dishonorable discharge, bad conduct discharge, or a discharge under other than honorable conditions may retain only nonrecoverable items that were issued prior to the individual being identified for separation or discharge. Civilian outer clothing is authorized per paragraph 12–9b.

b. Civilian outer clothing will be issued, if necessary, to all persons discharged for reasons as shown in paragraph 12–9a. The cost to the Government will not exceed $40 for each individual.

(1) Items of outer clothing for both male and female personnel will be of suitable civilian attire. Males are issued a shirt and trousers. Females are issued a skirt or slacks and blouse. A jacket is authorized when required for comfort during travel. When weather conditions warrant, wearing an all-weather coat is authorized. It may be procured from the AMCS when Condition Code B stock of the all-weather coat is available. The cost is 50 percent of the acquisition cost.

(2) Requests from USDB for civilian clothing are sent through the General Services Administration, using the federal supply schedules. If sizes are not available through federal supply schedules, local procurement is authorized.

(3) All other installations procure civilian clothing locally.

(4) Requests for funds for local procurement of civilian clothing will be sent through normal supply and command funding channels. The purchase of this clothing will be charged to OMA funds.

c. Prisoners in pretrial confinement and those sentenced to confinement only are transferred to the confinement facility with clothing items listed in table 5–4. The installation commander may establish local policy to limit the number of items authorized. The following procedures apply:

(1) Before departure to the confinement facility, the unit commander, or a designated representative, conducts a physical inventory and inspection of military clothing items in a prisoner's possession or control. Items are recorded on DA Form 3078. Safekeeping, inventorying, and use of DA Form 3078 are covered in paragraph 12–12. The inventorying officer signs all copies of the form. Disposition of the forms are as follows:

(a) The original copy is placed in the prisoner's IPERMS.

(b) The unit commander retains one copy.

(c) One copy is given to the prisoner for retention.

(d) When the prisoner is released and returned to duty, the original copy is sent with the individual's records to the unit of assignment. Shortages in initial issue clothing will be replaced at the expense of the Soldier upon returning to duty.

(2) Prisoners collecting the basic or standard monetary allowance will maintain prescribed clothing items at their own expense.

(3) The unit commander retains and secures for safekeeping any military clothing items not required at the confinement facility.

d. If a person is confined in a civilian confinement facility, the unit commander retains and secures items not to exceed one year. After the 1-year period, items are turned in through normal supply channels. The turn-in documents are placed in the prisoner's IPERMS.

e. Prisoners transferred to an Army correctional holding detachment are allowed outer clothing necessary for health and comfort during transport. The unit commander of prisoners whose sentences include a punitive discharge turns in all other military items of outer clothing. Nonrecoverable items are excluded.

12–10. Personal clothing receipt statement

a. All enlisted Soldiers being discharged or separated from Active Army service will read and sign the statement shown in table 12–2.

b. If the Soldier reenlists within 3 months, the list of items turned in will be used to provide an issue-in-kind of like items.

(1) This list may be prepared on DA Form 3078.

(2) An officer or warrant officer having knowledge of the items that were turned in will place a statement in DA Form 3078.

(3) The unit retains one copy of the DA Form 3078. This form will be filed in accordance with AR 25–400–2. One copy is placed in the Soldier's unit file and one copy is given to the Soldier.

c. Personnel who are REFRAD and transferred to ARNG or USAR, to include USAR control group, will sign the statement shown in table 12–3. This statement will be entered on the appropriate side of DA Form 4886. To ensure proper personal clothing accountability is established, commanders of the last unit of assignment or attachment will ensure that DA Form 4886, with the signed statement on the appropriate side, is prepared and placed in the Soldier's unit file.

d. Personnel, who are separated from ARNG or USAR units and transferred to USAR control groups for completion of their reserve obligation in accordance with AR 140–10 or National Guard Regulation 600–200, will be required to sign the statement shown in table 12–3. The original copy of the signed statement will be placed in the Soldier's unit file. In the event the Soldier is unavailable for signature, the unit commander will certify the quantities previously issued to the Soldier and in their possession. The commander's certificate will be attached to the Soldier's clothing records and placed in the Soldier's unit file prior to transfer.

e. Personnel who are being discharged from the Active Army and elect to immediately enlist in the ARNG or USAR, to include USAR control groups, will be required to sign the statement shown in table 12–3. The commander of the Soldier's last unit of assignment, or the separation point commander, for Soldiers returning from OCONUS for separation will complete the DA Form 4886 to establish accountability of uniforms in the Soldier's possession. The original copy of DA Form 4886 and the original copy of the signed statement will be placed in the Soldier's IPERMS.

Table 12–2
Statement of personal clothing receipt

Installation (Name) Date (Day, Month, Year)
The personal clothing listed on DA Form 3078 is currently in my possession.
Signed (Signature of person discharged or released)

Table 12–3
Clothing statement for enlisted Soldiers with a remaining reserve obligation

I (fill in name) understand that I am required to maintain all personal clothing items in my possession, as indicated on the DA Form 4886 in a serviceable condition until the expiration of my reserve obligation on (fill in date). I further understand that if I am mobilized as a Soldier of the reserves, I am required to bring all items on the attached form with me to my designated mobilization site. Failure to do this will result in me required to reimburse the Government for all missing items.

12–11. Nonretention of clothing

a. Soldiers discharged from active duty without a Reserve obligation may elect not to retain uniform items. This means forfeiture of future clothing entitlement after discharge or separation from the Service.

b. The installation commander will authorize an approved local request for non retention of military clothing. The individual signs the request and a commissioned or warrant officer confirms it. The signed request is filed in the Soldier's unit file.

12–12. Clothing items not authorized for retention

a. All basic issue clothing items (except organizational property such as patches and crests) will remain with the enlisted Soldier when they are transferred. The unit will ensure an accurate inventory is done prior to transfer as a part of the Soldier's out processing. The clothing record will be included in the Soldier's IPERMS (see para 14–9).

b. Clothing items not authorized for retention, are withdrawn, classified, and turned in to the supply system (see para 1–6*a*). If they are not required in the supply system, they are turned in to the DRMS. All ARNG items not authorized for retention are processed as prescribed by appendix C of the ARNG Central Clothing Distribution User Handbook.

12–13. Clothing of absentees

a. Inventory. The abandoned property of a Soldier absent from the unit without authority will be inventoried without delay following the procedures in paragraph 12–13*a*(1) and 12–13*a*(2). These procedures apply only if the enlisted Soldier resides in troop billets.

(1) The unit commander will designate a commissioned officer, warrant officer, or noncommissioned officer in pay grade E5 through E9 to conduct the inventory. The unit commander will assure the inventory officer that the clothing abandoned actually belongs to the absent enlisted Soldier. Another member of the unit or activity will witness this inventory.

(2) The inventory officer will—

(a) Make sure the clothing is not exchanged for clothing of any other enlisted Soldier.

(b) Prepare a DA Form 3078 in original and three copies. Record on this form the items and quantities of personal military clothing issued. Excesses of personal military clothing above authorized levels will not be recorded on DA Form 3078. These items will be included on the personal effects inventory. See DA Pam 600–8 for instructions on how privately owned military personal property is inventoried. The person conducting the inventory will enter the words "Inventoried by" and sign in the "Remarks" block of the DA Form 3078.

(c) Ensure that the witness and the unit commander or designated representative verify and initial this form.

(d) Place the original copy of the inventory in the enlisted Soldier's duffel bag or other suitable container. Retain the other three copies in the unit suspense file pending further action.

b. Safekeeping. Inventoried clothing of an absent enlisted Soldier discussed in paragraph 12–13*a* will be secured in the unit's facilities or in a secured storage area designated by the installation commander.

c. Return of the absent enlisted Soldier. Clothing is returned to the absentee. The enlisted Soldier will acknowledge receipt of the clothing by signing all copies of DA Form 3078. The enlisted Soldier will be given copy three of the inventory. The unit commander determines whether the enlisted Soldier has the initial allowances of personal clothing. Shortages are replaced at the enlisted Soldier's expense.

12–14. Clothing of enlisted Soldiers dropped from the rolls

Clothing of enlisted Soldiers who are absent without leave is inventoried, safeguarded, and retained in the unit facilities or other suitable storage area per paragraph 12–13. When the enlisted Soldier is returned to military custody or dropped from the rolls as a deserter, clothing is disposed of as follows:

a. If the absentee is returned to an installation other than their home station before being dropped from the rolls, the home station commander—

(1) Ships the abandoned clothes to the enlisted Soldier's new station if the enlisted Soldier will not be returned to the home station unit.

(2) Determines the expense to the Government for shipping the clothes.

(3) Forwards the information to the new station for collection of shipping expenses from the enlisted Soldier's pay.

b. When an enlisted Soldier is dropped from the rolls as a deserter, clothing is removed from the unit facilities or other secured areas. Recoverable items are turned in to the Installation Supply Division. The following information will be entered on the turn in document:

(1) Identity of the enlisted Soldier and their assigned unit.

(2) Statement that the enlisted Soldier was dropped from the rolls on a certain date.

(3) Statement that all abandoned recoverable items listed on DA Form 4886 are included.

c. The unit commander or representative, above the grade of E4, will inventory clothing of ARNG and USAR Soldiers dropped from the rolls.

(1) DA Form 4886, CCDF Form 3161, or CCDF Form 3078 will be prepared and accompany the clothing upon turn in. The turn in documents will—

(a) Identity of the enlisted Soldier and their assigned unit.

(b) Contain a statement that the enlisted Soldier was dropped from the rolls on a certain date.

(c) Contain a statement that all abandoned recoverable items listed on DA Form 4886 are included.

(2) The appropriate accountable officer (USPFO for ARNG) retains the original of the turn in document. One copy is sent to the Soldier's unit for filing. In the ARNG, a copy is sent to the State Adjutant General for inclusion in the Soldier's permanent file. All abandoned property in the ARNG is turned in to the USPFO per paragraph 15–10.

(3) Records are disposed of according to AR 25-400-2.

d. Clothing for Soldiers returned to military control after abandoned clothing has been disposed of is replaced at the Soldier's expense. This includes Soldiers of the ARNG and USAR.

e. According to AR 735–5, adjustment action will be taken for clothing not returned or recovered from ARNG Soldiers who are discharged or dropped from the rolls.

12–15. Clothing of hospitalized personnel

a. Hospitalized at duty installation. When an enlisted Soldier is hospitalized at a medical treatment facility at their duty installation, the following actions are taken:

(1) The facility commander, by the fastest means and within 24 hours after admission of the enlisted Soldier, will advise the unit commander.

(2) The unit commander, without delay, will have clothing and personal effects of the hospitalized person immediately secured and safeguarded in unit facilities or other secure areas.

(3) If the enlisted Soldier does not return within 120 hours, the clothing and personal effects will be inventoried according to paragraph 12–13.

b. Transferred to an off-post hospital. When an enlisted Soldier is to be transferred to a hospital away from their duty installation, the following procedures apply:

(1) The personal clothing will accompany the patient to the hospital, when possible. This applies to any Army, Navy, or Air Force hospital or local hospital servicing a military installation.

(2) The local medical facility commander will, by the fastest means, advise the unit commander of the transfer.

(3) If the enlisted Soldier has not returned to the unit within 72 hours, the unit commander will ensure that the enlisted Soldier's clothing is taken to the medical facility.

(4) The enlisted Soldier signs the unit's retained copy of DA Form 3078 to acknowledge receipt of the clothing. If the enlisted Soldier's physical condition prevents them from doing this, the medical facility commander designates an officer to acknowledge receipt of the clothing on behalf of the enlisted Soldier. This officer then makes certain the clothing accompanies the enlisted Soldier to the new hospital.

c. Transferred to medical holding detachment.

(1) On learning that an enlisted Soldier has been assigned to a medical holding detachment, the unit commander prepares a statement on letter-size paper. Format is shown in table 12–3.

Table 12–3
Statement of personal clothing belonging to person transferred to a medical detachment

The items and quantities of personal clothing belonging to (Name) (Last four of SSN) (Organization) and appearing on the attached DA Form 3078 were given to (Soldier's name) before transfer to (Name of medical detachment).

(2) The unit commander signs the statement. They will include on the statement their grade, unit, and organization. The statement is attached to a true copy of DA Form 3078 and retained in the unit's records.

d. Shipment of clothing.

(1) At times, emergencies make it physically impossible for the Soldier to take clothing with them on transfer to an off-post hospital. When this happens, the unit commander, within 24 hours after being informed of the transfer will—

(a) Have clothing shipped to the Soldier at Government expense.

(b) Place the original copy of DA Form 3078 in a secure container.

(c) Prepare a statement on letter size paper. A suggested format is shown in table 12–4.

Table 12–4
Statement of shipment of clothing

The items and quantities of personal clothing belonging to (Name) (Last four of SSN) (Organization) and appearing on the attached DA Form 3078 were shipped by (enter the Government bill of lading number) on (enter the date) by express, motor freight, or less than carload freight. (Cross out not applicable methods of shipment).

(d) Sign the statement. They will include on the statement their grade, and unit.

(e) Forward the statement and a copy of DA Form 3078 to the commanding officer of the medical holding company or detachment.

(2) If shipment is not received within a reasonable time, the commander of the medical holding company or detachment sends a tracer for the missing clothing. The tracer is sent to the enlisted Soldier's parent organization through the proper ACOM. If the clothing has been lost through no fault of the enlisted Soldier, the unit commander will furnish the hospital a true copy of DA Form 3078. Items of personal clothing shown on the form are replaced gratuitously.

12–16. Clothing of enlisted personnel on ordinary or emergency leave, temporary duty, or pass

a. Safekeeping. Each enlisted Soldier is responsible for safekeeping all clothing and equipment not accompanying them during authorized absences.

b. Storage. The unit commander will provide necessary storage facilities for enlisted Soldier's use, during authorized absences.

c. Transferred to another unit while on emergency leave or temporary duty. An enlisted Soldier may be transferred to another unit while on emergency leave or temporary duty. After receiving this information, the unit commander will, without delay, cause all applicable inventories of military and personal effects to be conducted in accordance with DA Pam 600–8 and DA Pam 710–2–1. Military clothing and personal effects will be shipped to the enlisted Soldier at Government expense. Exclude OCIE not authorized for retention.

d. Army National Guard of the United States and U.S. Army Reserve Soldiers. Soldiers of the ARNG and USAR are required to secure their individual clothing when the Armory or Center facilities are not made available by the unit commander.

12–17. Abandoned and unclaimed clothing in laundries and dry-cleaning plants

a. U.S. Army laundries and dry-cleaning plants. Some uniform clothing items are abandoned or left unclaimed in Army laundries and dry-cleaning plants. Items are dropped from laundry accountable records after 90 days, per AR 210–130.

b. Commercial establishments. Army funds will not be expended to recover unclaimed and abandoned clothing bag items from commercial facilities. If items are voluntarily returned to an Army installation without reimbursement, the clothing becomes the property of the Government and is processed through normal channels.

c. Gratuitous issue. Gratuitous issue of clothing authorized by paragraph 5–4 is not authorized to Soldiers abandoning clothing and footwear.

d. Deceased personnel. See AR 638–2.

12–18. Unclaimed repaired or altered clothing left in Government or commercial facilities

a. Articles of personal clothing left by Soldiers in Government clothing repair shops for alteration or repair are considered abandoned after 120 days. Abandoned clothing is turned in through normal supply channels.

b. Articles of personal clothing left by officer or enlisted Soldiers in commercial concessions for alteration or repair will be disposed of in accordance with paragraph 12–17*b.*

12–19. Deceased personnel

a. Authority for obtaining Army service uniform and component items for burial of eligible deceased military Soldiers is found in AR 638–2.

b. Procedures for the withdrawal of clothing and equipment from deceased Soldiers, is found in see AR 638–2.

c. The mortuary office or mortuary affairs coordinator will—

(1) Take an ASU from the Soldier's personal effects if it is in a serviceable condition. If an ASU cannot be found, one will be issued by the AMCS or purchased locally at Government expense.

(2) Prepare a DA Form 3078 according to paragraph 5–2 showing the items of military clothing required. The appropriate base operation accounting classification will be placed in the remarks block quoting disposition of remains funds as chargeable for reimbursement. The mortuary officer or mortuary affairs coordinator may approve the DA Form 3078 pertaining to the burial of deceased active duty Soldiers. This document will be hand carried to the AMCS manager who will process the issue.

(3) Request insignia, awards, and decorations on DA Form 2765–1 through normal supply channels.

Chapter 13
Alterations

13–1. Alterations at government expense

Alterations to personal clothing at Government expense are limited to authorized outer items. Alterations will be made—

a. At the time of issue or sale (all cash and individual charge sales to enlisted Soldiers).

b. On receipt of uniform items obtained through mail order purchases.

c. During the first 6 months (180 days) of service under the clothing allowance system when outer clothing becomes too small or too large because of major changes in height or weight.

d. When on the issue-in-kind system. (ARNG and USAR pays for alterations)

e. At any time damage is not the fault of the enlisted Soldier (see para 5–11).

f. USAR and Army National Guard of the United States enlisted Soldiers in remote sites are authorized local alterations (see para 14–19).

13–2. Alterations at enlisted Soldier's expense

Under circumstances other than those in paragraph 13–1, alterations are made at the Soldier's own expense, such as Exchange commercially procured uniforms. Alterations may be made in commercial facilities or in Government operated clothing repair facilities. If Government facilities are used, the following conditions apply:

a. The clothing repair facility is physically located at the Army installation.

b. The workload in the repair facility permits use of the facilities for this purpose.

c. No additional personnel are necessary to do the work.

13–3. Facilities available to officers and warrant officers

Army commissioned officers and warrant officers may use the clothing repair facility for the alteration of individual clothing at the discretion of the post commander. The type and quality of work is the same for both enlisted Soldiers and officers. Alteration service is extended to enlisted Soldiers before officer personnel when the workload in the repair facility does not permit use of facilities at the same time. Alteration services rendered for officer personnel are at the expense of the officer.

13–4. Authorized alterations

Authorized alterations to clothing are shown in tables 13–1 and 13–2. Also, USAR and ARNG enlisted Soldiers in remote sites are authorized local alterations (see para 14–19).

Table 13–1
Authorized alterations for men's uniforms

Item: Coat, all weather, black
Alteration: Sleeves, hemline

Item: Trousers[1]
Alteration: Bottoms, crotch, seat, waist

Item: Coat
Alteration: Shoulders, collar, sleeves, side or back seams, hemline, button alignment, back waist length, sleeves ornamental braids adjustment

Item: Shirt (long sleeves and short sleeves)
Alteration: Sleeves[2], back or side seams

Notes:
[1] Alterations to uniforms, ACU are limited to shortening the trouser length. Alterations will be done in accordance with TM 10–227.
[2] The long sleeves of the ASU shirt can be shortened only if they are one inch or more excess length. The buttons on cuffs may be set over. Alterations will be done in accordance with TM 10–227.

Table 13–2
Authorized alterations to women's uniforms

Item: Coat, all weather, black
Alteration: Sleeves, hemline

Item: Coat
Alteration: Shoulders, collar, sleeves, back or side seams, back waist length, hemline, button alignment, bust, sleeves ornamental braids adjustment

Item: Skirt
Alteration: Waist, hemline

Item: Slacks
Alteration: Back or side seams, bottoms, crotch, seat, waist

Item: Shirt, Cotton and/or poly, Tuck In, Shade #521
Alteration: Sleeves[1] back or side seams

Notes:
[1] The long sleeves of the ASU shirt can be shortened only if they are one inch or more excess length. The buttons on cuffs may be set over. Alterations will be done in accordance with TM 10–227.

13–5. Wounded Warrior Clothing Support Program for U.S. Army Medical Command Wounded Warrior transition units

a. The MTF where the Wounded Warrior (WW) is recovering will provide necessary adaptive clothing while on inpatient and outpatient status. Adaptive clothing includes items such as, shorts, shirts, undergarments to accommodate for tubing, amputation, burns, and other injuries.

b. When a WW enlisted Soldier or officer is evacuated to a medical treatment facility because of injuries or illness, the medical treatment commander will authorize sufficient uniform clothing on a gratuitous basis to meet the Soldier's needs (see table 5–1).

c. A gratuitous clothing issue will be authorized for WWs who are being provided medical treatment on an outpatient basis, assigned to the WTU, and are in a medical hold status.

d. The gratuitous clothing issue request DA Form 3078 requirement will be completed within 30 days of the WW being assigned to the MTF unless there are medical reasons or other circumstances that prevented the WW from receiving clothing earlier. This is a one-time gratuitous clothing issue based on the WW emergency medical evacuation from theater.

e. WWs, officers, and enlisted who continued on active duty (COAD) and continued on Active Reserve (COAR) are authorized to receive additional clothing bag items when prescribed by an occupational therapist (OT) or physical therapist (PT) as outlined in paragraphs 13–6d(1) through 13–6d(3).

f. Medical OT or PT personnel will provide a written statement memorandum supporting the reason why the WW did not receive clothing within 30 days.

g. The remarks block will have the following statement added, "Operation ENDURING FREEDOM emergency evacuated from theater. Individual has not received a full or partial gratuitous clothing issue while in the Wounded Warrior Clothing Support Program."

13–6. Wounded Warrior Clothing Support Program clothing modification and alterations procedures

The WWCSP provides Army WWs the ability to have their military clothing items modified or altered for wear depending on the extent of the injuries sustained as a result of combat operations and special footwear (commercial boots, athletic shoes, and shoes) as prescribed by the OT or PT. These services are provided to the WWs at no cost to Active Army Soldiers who continue on active duty, active USAR Soldiers, active ARNG Soldiers, continued-on-active-Reserve Soldiers, and fit-for-duty Soldiers.

 a. Soldiers requiring uniform modification or alterations must have a DA Form 3078 personal clothing request with the uniform measurements prescribed by an OT or PT. The DA Form 3078 will be signed by unit commander.

 b. Soldiers will take their uniforms and completed DA Form 3078 to the Exchange alteration concessionaire. The Exchange concessionaire will perform the requested service to meet the OT or PT guidelines for the Soldier's need. The alteration work on the Soldier's uniform is completed and ready for pickup in approximately 3 to 5 business days.

 c. Soldiers requiring special commercial footwear must have a prescription from an OT or PT and signed by unit commander.

Note. OT or PT clinics at MTFs may purchase commercial footwear or commanders can locally purchase using a Government purchase card (OMA funds).

 d. COAD, COAR, and fit-for-duty Soldiers (enlisted and officers) will obtain required clothing bag (CB) items as prescribed by the OT or PT as follows:

 (1) COAD or fit-for-duty Soldiers will continue to receive their CRA to procure CB items from the AMCS.

 (2) COAR or fit-for-duty Army enlisted Soldiers will continue to receive their CRA CB items using the issued-in-kind process from the KYLOC.

 (3) COAD, COAR, and fit-for-duty officers (Active Army, USAR, and ARNG) will receive CB items using the gratuitous issue program, personal clothing request, on DA Form 3078 submitted to the AMCS.

 e. The WWCSP provides CB items and free modification or alterations to WWs that are in transition, recovery, training, and return-to-duty status (COAD, COAR, and fit-for-duty Soldiers).

13–7. Wounded Warrior Clothing Support Program alterations criteria

 a. Alterations to all uniform and clothing items must be designed to fit as best as possible while also ensuring functionality is maintained without significantly changing the outward appearance of the uniform. Following are some ways clothing may be modified or altered by the alteration facility:

 (1) Change fastening systems. Replace buttons with hook and loop, laces, or zippers.

 (2) Tailor the uniform and clothing to provide the Soldier a proper fit based on medical profile or condition.

 (3) Use velcro or other attachments on the uniform, trouser or slacks legs, or shirt or coat sleeves because of limb amputation or other medical profile conditions.

 b. When modification or alterations are required in areas without an Exchange concessionaire MEDCOM will pay for local modification and alterations as prescribed by the OT or PT.

13–8. Unauthorized alterations

Alterations will not be made if they—

 a. Cause a material change from the approved concept of fit of the garment.

 b. Change a garment to about the same size as another standard tariff garment, unless size substitutions are made by the source of supply.

Chapter 14
Issue-In-Kind System for U.S. Army Reserve Personal Clothing

Section I
U.S. Army Reserve Central Clothing Distribution Facility

14–1. Extension of central clothing distribution facility
The DLA–TS has extended the contractor-operated CCDF to serve USAR customers.

14–2. Mission
The mission of the CCDF is to provide USAR enlisted Soldiers authorized issue-in-kind with their total requirements for military clothing, including insignia and decorations, from a single location. Ordering is primarily via the Web site at http://www.kyloc.com with other options for units lacking Internet access. Requests for CCDF Web site access are

processed through the Army Reserve. Orders are configured and shipped directly to units in Soldier kits with name and Army tapes, as applicable, affixed.

Section II
Central Clothing Distribution Facility

14–3. Inventories
The CCDF inventory of new material is owned by DLA–TS. The USAR is billed monthly for issues to their units during the previous month. The billing and billing validation processes are described in the CCDF management plan.

14–4. Sale of clothing by the central clothing distribution facility
Only individuals authorized issue-in-kind are supported by the CCDF. The CCDF does not make cash or credit sales. Individuals may purchase needed clothing from AMCS facilities or the Exchange (Internet or mail order sales options), see chapter 12.

Section II
Issue-in-Kind for U.S. Army Reserve Personal Clothing

14–5. Introduction
The issue-in-kind for personal clothing, when authorized by the Secretary of the Army, is accounted for on DA Form 4886. Figure 14–1 shows a sample of a completed DA Form 4886 and instructions for completing the form.

ISSUE-IN-KIND-PERSONAL CLOTHING RECORD

For use of this form, see AR 700-84; the proponent agency is DCS, G-4

DATA REQUIRED BY THE PRIVACY ACT OF 1974

AUTHORITY: 5 U.S.C. Section 301, Department Regulations; 10 U.S.C. Section 3013, Secretary of the Army; Army Regulation 700-84, Issue and Sale of Personal Clothing; and E.O. 9397 as amended.

PRINCIPAL PURPOSE: The issue-in-kind personal clothing records provide an accountable document for clothing received by Reserve Component enlisted Soldier.

ROUNTINE USES: The information furnished is used solely for the purpose of identifying the individual so that the clothing record will be filed in the correct Military Personnel Records Jacket and will not be shared with agencies outside of DoD. The DoD Blanket Routine Uses that appear at the beginning of the Army's compilation of systems of records may apply to this system.

DISCLOSURE: Voluntary. However, failure to provide all the request information will prevent from receiving the allocated clothing.

THIS IS A PERMANENT RECORD

NAME *(Last, First, MI)* GRADE AND SSN (Last four)
Doe, John T.   PVT   1234

INSTRUCTIONS:
Entries in ink: Name, Rank, SSN (Last four), Quantity, Date, and Signature.
Columns 1 thru 15 are used for recording consecutive clothing inventories.

PERSONAL CLOTHING ITEMS *(Common)*	SIZE	AUTH ALW	1	2	3	4	5	6	7	8	9	10	11	12	13	14	15
Bag, Duffle Nylon Improved	------	1	1	-	-	-	-	-	-	-	-	-	-	-	-	-	-
Belt, Riggers	------	1	1	-	-	-	-	-	-	-	-	-	-	-	-	-	-
Beret, Wool Black Shade 1593	7	1	1	-	-	-	-	-	-	-	-	-	-	-	-	-	-
Boot, Combat, HW, Tan OR	10R	1	1	-	-	-	-	-	-	-	-	-	-	-	-	-	-
Boot, Combat, TW, Type II, Tan	10R	1	1	-	-	-	-	-	-	-	-	-	-	-	-	-	-
Cap, Patrol, Army Combat Uniform	7 1/4	2	2	-	-	-	-	-	-	-	-	-	-	-	-	-	-
Cap, Synthetic Micro Fleece	------	1	1	-	-	-	-	-	-	-	-	-	-	-	-	-	-
Coat, Army Combat Uniform	MR	4	4	-	-	-	-	-	-	-	-	-	-	-	-	-	-
Gloves, Light Duty Utility	M	1	1	-	-	-	-	-	-	-	-	-	-	-	-	-	-
Gloves, Inserts, Cold, Foliage	6	2	2	-	-	-	-	-	-	-	-	-	-	-	-	-	-
Gloves, Leather, Black, Unisex	6	1	1	-	-	-	-	-	-	-	-	-	-	-	-	-	-
Jacket, PFU	L	1	1	-	-	-	-	-	-	-	-	-	-	-	-	-	-
Pants, PFU	XL	1	1	-	-	-	-	-	-	-	-	-	-	-	-	-	-
Shirt, L/S, PFU	L	1	1	-	-	-	-	-	-	-	-	-	-	-	-	-	-
Shirt, S/S, PFU	L	2	2	-	-	-	-	-	-	-	-	-	-	-	-	-	-
Sock, Boot	M	7	7	-	-	-	-	-	-	-	-	-	-	-	-	-	-
Sock, Liner, Poly/Nylon, Black	M	7	7	-	-	-	-	-	-	-	-	-	-	-	-	-	-
Trousers, Army Combat Uniform	MR	4	4	-	-	-	-	-	-	-	-	-	-	-	-	-	-
Trunks, PFU	L	2	2	-	-	-	-	-	-	-	-	-	-	-	-	-	-
T-Shirt, Moisture-Wick	L	7	7	-	-	-	-	-	-	-	-	-	-	-	-	-	-

DA FORM 4886, MAY 2014   EDITION OF MAY 93 IS OBSOLETE   APD LF v1.00

Figure 14–1. Example of a completed DA Form 4886

ISSUE-IN-KIND-PERSONAL CLOTHING RECORD

For use of this form, see AR 700-84; the proponent agency is DCS, G-4

DATA REQUIRED BY THE PRIVACY ACT OF 1974

AUTHORITY: 5 U.S.C. Section 301, Department Regulations; 10 U.S.C. Section 3013, Secretary of the Army; Army Regulation 700-84, Issue and Sale of Personal Clothing; and E.O. 9397 as amended.

PRINCIPAL PURPOSE: The issue-in-kind personal clothing records provide an accountable document for clothing received by Reserve Component enlisted Soldier.

ROUNTINE USES: The information furnished is used solely for the purpose of identifying the individual so that the clothing record will be filed in the correct Military Personnel Records Jacket and will not be shared with agencies outside of DoD. The DoD Blanket Routine Uses that appear at the beginning of the Army's compilation of systems of records may apply to this system.

DISCLOSURE: Voluntary. However, failure to provide all the request information will prevent from receiving the allocated clothing.

THIS IS A PERMANENT RECORD

NAME *(Last, First, MI)* GRADE AND SSN (Last four)
Doe, John T. PVT   1234

INSTRUCTIONS:
Entries in ink: Name, Rank, SSN (Last four), Quantity, Date, and Signature.
Columns 1 thru 15 are used for recording consecutive clothing inventories.

PERSONAL CLOTHING ITEMS (Common)	SIZE	AUTH ALW	1	2	3	4	5	6	7	8	9	10	11	12	13	14	15
Bag, Duffle Nylon Improved	------	1	1	-	-	-	-	-	-	-	-	-	-	-	-	-	-
Belt, Riggers	------	1	1	-	-	-	-	-	-	-	-	-	-	-	-	-	-
Beret, Wool Black Shade 1593	7	1	1	-	-	-	-	-	-	-	-	-	-	-	-	-	-
Boot, Combat, HW, Tan OR	10R	1	1	-	-	-	-	-	-	-	-	-	-	-	-	-	-
Boot, Combat, TW, Type II, Tan	10R	1	1	-	-	-	-	-	-	-	-	-	-	-	-	-	-
Cap, Patrol, Army Combat Uniform	7 1/4	2	2	-	-	-	-	-	-	-	-	-	-	-	-	-	-
Cap, Synthetic Micro Fleece	------	1	1	-	-	-	-	-	-	-	-	-	-	-	-	-	-
Coat, Army Combat Uniform	MR	4	4	-	-	-	-	-	-	-	-	-	-	-	-	-	-
Gloves, Light Duty Utility	M	1	1	-	-	-	-	-	-	-	-	-	-	-	-	-	-
Gloves, Inserts, Cold, Foliage	6	2	2	-	-	-	-	-	-	-	-	-	-	-	-	-	-
Gloves, Leather, Black, Unisex	6	1	1	-	-	-	-	-	-	-	-	-	-	-	-	-	-
Jacket, PFU	L	1	1	-	-	-	-	-	-	-	-	-	-	-	-	-	-
Pants, PFU	XL	1	1	-	-	-	-	-	-	-	-	-	-	-	-	-	-
Shirt, L/S, PFU	L	1	1	-	-	-	-	-	-	-	-	-	-	-	-	-	-
Shirt, S/S, PFU	L	2	2	-	-	-	-	-	-	-	-	-	-	-	-	-	-
Sock, Boot	M	7	7	-	-	-	-	-	-	-	-	-	-	-	-	-	-
Sock, Liner, Poly/Nylon, Black	M	7	7	-	-	-	-	-	-	-	-	-	-	-	-	-	-
Trousers, Army Combat Uniform	MR	4	4	-	-	-	-	-	-	-	-	-	-	-	-	-	-
Trunks, PFU	L	2	2	-	-	-	-	-	-	-	-	-	-	-	-	-	-
T-Shirt, Moisture-Wick	L	7	7	-	-	-	-	-	-	-	-	-	-	-	-	-	-

DA FORM 4886, MAY 2014   EDITION OF MAY 93 IS OBSOLETE   APD LF v1.00

Figure 14–1. Example of a completed DA Form 4886–continued

a. Entitlements to initial personal clothing allowances are discussed in chapter 4. Replacement of clothing is on a one to one basis, such as boots for boots, or ACUs for ACUs. Minimum usage criteria under which clothing exchanges are authorized is established as 3 years from date of initial issue. Exceptions must be authorized by the unit commander. Replacement clothing is clothing issued to replace lost, damaged, or destroyed clothing. If due to FWT and not to fault or negligence of the individual, the replacement clothing is free. If due to fault or negligence, replacement is at the individual's expense.

b. Exchanged or surplus items will be turned in to the support installation for disposition. Prior to turn-in of clothing to the supply system—

(1) Make proper entries to the expendable or durable document register.

(2) Remove quantities turned in from the Soldier's DA Form 4886.

(3) Place a copy of the turn-in document in the individual's personal clothing record file.

c. All requests for initial issue or replacement of personal clothing, except for ASU insignia and name plates, will be made using a CCDF Form 3078. The form will be completed using the online CCDF 3078 System. To access the system, follow the instructions provided in paragraph 1–4g(1). CCDF Form 3078 will be prepared on an individual basis and filed in accordance with AR 25–400–2. It will be entered in the expendable or durable document register and a copy retained as a suspense document, processed through the CCDF at http://www.kyloc.com. Upon receipt of clothing, items will be posted to the expendable or durable document register and the Soldier's DA Form 4886. A copy of the CCDF Form 3078 will be retained in the supporting document file for 2 years. Personal clothing will not be stocked in unit supply rooms. Personal clothing held in the supply room pending issue or turn-in (serviceable or unserviceable) will be tagged with the enlisted Soldier's full name, rank, and last four of the Soldier's SSN. Inventory of personal clothing for try-on is not authorized. Appropriate measurement procedures are contained in TM 10–227. Clothing and footwear sizing information are contained in SB 10–523. Detailed procedures in these publications will be followed as closely as possible to avoid ordering wrong sizes.

d. Insignia, nameplates, and nametapes are ordered through normal supply channels, using DA Form 2765–1. Multiple requests for nameplates or nametapes may be ordered using a single DA Form 2765–1 with an attached alphabetical name roster. Insignias may be stocked in unit supply rooms and issued as required per paragraph 5–5.

e. ACU nametapes, rank insignia, Army tapes, and U.S. Flags are requested from the CCDF.

14–6. Requests for personal clothing

a. Requests for personal clothing are submitted using CCDF Form 3078 at http://www.kyloc.com. Requests for personal clothing will not be consolidated. One request will be completed for each individual, whether for initial or replacement issue. Approving authority for individual orders will be the commander or their representative. Ordering official and approving official should not be the same individual.

b. USAR units are responsible for ensuring Soldiers possess all CB items prior to attending advanced individual training. Initial issues for prior service Soldiers will be made following the procedures above. Recruiters must ensure all Soldiers are properly in-processed with the USAR unit prior to any school attendance. Ample time must be allowed for the issue of uniforms.

c. On receipt of items, the unit will—

(1) Make proper entries to the expendable or durable document register.

(2) Post-quantities of personal clothing received to the Soldier's DA Form 4886 per paragraph 14–5. Retain per DA Pam 25–403.

14–7. Inventory of personal clothing upon receipt

Upon receipt of personal clothing, whether by mail from the CCDF or issued at the AMCS, supply personnel receiving the clothing will immediately inventory the items against the CCDF Form 3078 or AMCS annotated DA Form 3078. If the inventory matches the issued quantity, the person receiving the clothing will sign DA Form 3078, block 31 or CCDF Form 3078. This will be maintained on the Soldier's DA Form 4886 per paragraph 14–5.

14–8. Army Reserve Soldiers ordered to annual training or service schools

a. Soldiers ordered to AT, active duty for training, or service schools (179 days or fewer) normally have their required or authorized clothing prior to reporting for training. Soldiers who are short of clothing items may draw from the AMCS at their training site. The following procedures apply:

(1) *Unit Soldiers.*

(a) The unit commander will provide a letter stating the Soldier has not received clothing items needed for training.

(b) The unit supply representative will prepare a DA Form 3078 in accordance with paragraph 1–6*p*.

(c) The DA Form 3078 will be processed through the AMCS to the CSO for authorization and payment.

(d) The Soldier reports to AMCS to receive requested items.

(2) *Individual ready reserve or individual mobilization augmentee Soldiers.* See paragraphs 14–16 and 14–17. The school commandant or training unit commander will determine the uniform requirements for course attendance or unit training and complete the DA Form 3078 (see fig 3–1).

b. AMCS will process the requests.

c. The following statement will be placed on the front of the DA Form 3078: "I understand that the uniforms issued to me as indicated on the front of DA Form 3078 must be maintained in a serviceable condition by me until the end of my reserve obligation. In addition, I am required to be in possession of these uniforms for all future training periods or upon reporting to my designated mobilization site in the event the reserve forces are mobilized. Failure to do this will result in my being required to reimburse the Government for any missing uniform items." Statement to be followed by the individual's signature, rank, last four of SSN, and date signed.

d. AMCS will process requests on a fill or kill basis.

e. A copy of DA Form 3078 and the Soldier's signed statement will be placed in unit file and forwarded to the enlisted Soldier's home station. The unit supply personnel will requisition any shortages from the CCDF. Unit supply personnel will process statement of charges in accordance with AR 735–5 for all items previously issued that the Soldier failed to take to the training site. Personal clothing issued in excess of reserve allowances, in accordance with CTA 50–900, USAR–RPA, will not be withdrawn from the Soldier; however, issue-in-kind replacements are not authorized until the reserve allowances are met.

f. It is the unit commander's responsibility to ensure that issues are properly posted to Soldier's DA Form 4886.

14–9. Accounting for personal clothing

a. Unit or activity commanders will ensure that Soldiers have in their possession at all times, and in a serviceable condition, all items posted to their clothing records. Commanders will conduct inspections or inventories of personal clothing annually to ensure that all items are on hand and serviceable.

b. Authentication of annual clothing inventory or inspection will be recorded as follows:

(1) The quantity on hand will be recorded in the next available column of DA Form 4886. The authentication will be "PER INV," dated and signed in the signature or date block of DA Form 4886 by the individual conducting the inventory and/or inspection. If nonsupply personnel are conducting the inventory or inspection, they will be at least one grade higher than the individual being inspected.

(2) For items that are not serviceable because of FWT, a turn-in will be initiated and a replacement will be immediately requested. An adjustment document, in accordance with AR 735–5, will be initiated for those items that are short or unserviceable because of individual neglect.

(3) Commanders may permit corporals through sergeants major to furnish a statement, as shown in table 1–2 that they have all personal clothing items and all items are serviceable.

c. Replacement of clothing is authorized when—

(1) Personal clothing becomes unserviceable through FWT (see para 14–1*b*).

(2) Soldier has a weight variance as a result of a medically approved weight control program as prescribed in AR 600–9.

(3) It becomes unserviceable (destroyed or lost) through no fault of the individual.

(4) It is destroyed by order of a medical officer.

(5) It is destroyed by a natural disaster, such as fire or flood.

d. The following actions are taken when a new DA Form 4886 is required:

(1) The previous balances are posted in the first column. The unused blocks in the column are ruled out in ink. The date and signature of the person are placed at the bottom of the column. The old DA Form 4886 is retained in accordance with AR 25–400–2.

(2) If DA Form 4886 is lost, the unit commander directs that an inventory of personal clothing be taken. Quantities of items in laundries or in repair shops are counted as inventories on hand. Based on this inventory, a new DA Form 4886 is prepared. The new form is annotated in the remarks block: Replaces lost form. Quantities on hand within authorized allowances are placed in column 1. Items less than the allowance are replaced at the Soldier's expense unless they prove that the items were never issued.

14–10. Accounting for personal clothing when Soldiers are released from initial active duty for training

a. When Soldier returns from IADT, USAR unit, or activity commanders will ensure that personal clothing issued at reception or training center has been posted to DA Form 4886. This posting will be completed no later than the second battle assembly after Soldier returns from IADT.

b. Issues made at the reception or training center on DA Form 3078, will be posted to the Soldier's DA Form 4886 and retained in the individual clothing record, per AR 25–400–2. If a DA Form 3078 is not received from the training center, initial postings to the DA Form 4886 will be made from the results of a clothing inventory.

c. If clothing becomes unserviceable due to FWT, replacements, not to exceed authorized allowances, are made.

d. When there is a lack of clothing and the clothing record shows that items were issued, Soldiers must replace them at their own expense or sign a statement of charges.

14–11. Accounting for personal clothing when members are released from active duty with a reserve contractual obligation

a. Soldiers having a contractual obligation will bring all of their personal clothing with them when they report for their first training assembly. This includes Soldiers arriving after release from active duty and those reporting from the USAR control group.

b. Prepare a DA Form 3078 for all replacement and initial issue shortages. The DA Form 3078 will be placed in the Soldier's IPERMS prior to the Soldier departing for their ADOS assignment. Upon arrival at ADOS assignment station, the ADOS commander will sign and date the new DA Form 3078 for the shortage items. The Soldier will hand carry the DA Form 3078 to the AMCS for issue of the clothing items.

(1) During the first battle assembly a 100 percent showdown inventory will be conducted of all personal clothing in the Soldier's possession. The inventory will be recorded on the Soldier's DA Form 4886 and annotated "No DA Form 3078, account established by inventory."

(2) If the prior service Soldier has all required personal clothing issued from active duty, only the reserve allowance will be accounted for on the DA Form 4886.

(3) When the Soldier's file arrives and the DA Form 3078 or DA Form 4886 reflects that items were issued but not accounted for during the initial inventory, supply personnel will advise the Soldier that replacement will be at the Soldier's expense. This may be accomplished by the Soldier going to AMCS and purchasing the missing items, or unit supply personnel initiating a DD Form 362, in accordance with AR 735–5.

(4) If the Soldier elects to use the DD Form 362, the DA Form 3078 will be marked replacement. Supply personnel will enter in the remarks block (block 30) the following statement: "Statement of charges document number xxxx-xxxx" and fund cite.

14–12. Accounting for personal clothing on change of status

a. When the assignment or duty station of a Soldier changes within or between RCs, the personal clothing record will be transferred to the gaining organization. All personal clothing, to include supplemental items in CTA 50–900 will remain in the possession of the Soldier. USAR Soldiers will not be permitted to hand carry clothing records to new unit assignment.

b. USAR Soldiers discharged to accept a commission or warrant officer appointment will retain authorized items of clothing in their possession at the time of appointment. Obsolete or unserviceable items will not be replaced. DA Form 4886 will be closed out and annotated with the remark: "Soldier discharged to accept a commission or warrant officer appointment (as applicable). Records will be maintained in accordance with AR 25–400–2."

c. Soldiers who have or have not satisfactorily completed their obligation or enlistment will retain all personal clothing on separation.

d. The DA Form 4886 for Soldiers being separated from the unit and transferred to a USAR control group for completion of their reserve obligation will be processed according to the procedures in paragraph 12–10 and table 12–1. A copy of the Soldier's DA Form 4886 and transfer orders will be maintained at the losing unit in the Soldier issue file for 2 years.

e. Soldiers who are leaving a troop program unit to come on special active duty for training will retain all personal clothing. Personal clothing authorization for special active duty for training personnel is the same as active duty levels.

14–13. Processing turn-ins of personal clothing

When no requirement exists, personal clothing is turn-in to the DRMS at the supporting installation. Accounting procedures will be established to ensure that the turned in of personal clothing, if appropriate, is credited to the proper appropriation. Items of personal clothing unique to the ROTC program will be turned in to the installation supply division at the supporting installation. In the USAR, turn-ins and requests for replacement of personal clothing items will be processed in the following manner:

a. All personal clothing turned in by, or withdrawn from Soldiers, will be turned in to the installation turn-in point on the appropriate documents at the supporting installation. A document number will be assigned to the turn-in document from the expendable or durable document register.

b. When a replacement is requested and the Soldier does not turn in a like item or have a statement from the commander for a size change, and a review of their clothing record shows that an initial issue was made, the appropriate adjustment document will be initiated per AR 735–5.

c. In addition to the supply officer and supply sergeant, turn-ins may be acknowledged by civilian unit administrators or any commissioned or warrant officer designated, in writing, by the unit commander.

14–14. Personal clothing for U.S. Army Reserve Soldiers departing for 30 days or more of active duty for operational support

Prior to Soldiers departing for 30 days or more ADOS, the unit commander will—

a. Conduct a 100 percent personal clothing showdown inspection and record the results of the inspection in the next available column of DA Form 4886. This column will be annotated "INV," dated and signed by the unit commander or their designated representative. When clothing that was previously issued is missing, an adjustment document, in accordance with AR 735–5, will be initiated for the missing items prior to the Soldier departing for the ADOS assignment.

b. Prepare a DA Form 3078 for all replacement and initial issue shortages, up to the USAR allowances. The DA Form 3078 will be placed in the Soldier's IPERMS prior to the Soldier departing for their active duty for operational support assignment. Upon arrival at ADOS assignment station, the ADOS commander will sign and date the new DA Form 3078 for the shortage items. The gaining unit will process the request through the CCDF or, when the unit does not have CCDF access, the Soldier will hand carry the DA Form 3078 to the AMCS for issue of the clothing items.

c. Ensure that the Soldier's DA Form 4886 is placed in the unit file for forwarding to the ADOS assignment station, retaining a copy for the Soldier's personal clothing record file.

14–15. Personal clothing for U.S. Army Reserve individual ready reserve Soldiers

a. The commander of the attached training unit or reserve component activity commander at the supporting installation will—

(1) Inventory the uniform items in the Soldier's possession (if any) when reporting for training, using DA Form 3078 or DA Form 4886. This inventory will be verified by the unit commander, supply officer, or Directorate Reserve Component Support (DRCS).

(2) Determine any additional uniform item requirements based on their training orders and unit's scheduled training. The minimum amount of personal clothing considered essential by the attached unit commander or DRCS for completing IRR training requirements will be requested. The issue of ASUs and component items will be made only if required for the performance of duty or if the training orders indicate the Soldier is requested to complete an official DA photo in accordance with AR 640–30 while on training.

(3) Prepare an additional DA Form 3078 in six copies and annotate USAR and IRR in the category block. For IRR or IMA Soldiers, put the following statement in block 30, "Authorized by HRC (AHRC–ALL–S), Fort Knox, KY, 40121-5205." The sixth copy of DA Form 3078 is maintained by the requesting activity as a suspense copy.

(4) The Soldier will be required to sign the statement as shown in paragraph 14–8.

b. The IRR Soldier will take the original and four copies of DA Form 3078 to the AMCS for issue of personal clothing. AMCS issues the clothing and retains the original and three copies. The fifth copy is given to the Soldier as a receipt. If additional copies are needed, they will be provided by the unit commander or the DRCS.

(1) AMCS will process the requests on a case by case basis. Procedures for processing the clothing request are in chapter 5. Funds are charged to RPA.

(2) The unit commander will forward one copy of each DA Form 3078 containing the statement in paragraph 14–9b(3), and a copy of the Soldier's training orders to Commander, HRC, Fort Knox (AHRC–ALL–S), 1600 Spearhead Division Avenue, Fort Knox, KY, 40121–5205.

c. On completion of training, Soldiers will retain all clothing items.

d. IRR Soldiers attached to units or other DA organizations in an IDT without pay status (points only) may be issued uniforms as required for the performance of such training as in paragraph 14–16. The approval authority for such issue is the commander of the unit of attachment.

e. Exchange of obsolete or damaged uniforms may be made as discussed in paragraph 14–18.

14–16. Issue-in-kind for individual ready reserve or individual mobilization augmentation Soldiers

a. Replacement of obsolete, damaged items due to FWT will be made as follows:

(1) Obsolete or damaged uniforms will be turned in to the unit supply. Unit supply sergeant will prepare DA Form 3078 for replacement of the items in accordance with paragraph 1–6p. For IRR or IMA Soldiers, put the following statement in block 30, "Authorized by HRC (AHRC–ALL–S), Fort Knox, KY 40121–5205."

(2) The Soldier will report to AMCS for issue of the items.

(3) The AMCS will process the request on a case by case basis and retain the original and three copies. The Soldier will retain one copy and furnish the unit commander with two copies of the DA Form 3078.

(4) IMA unit commanders will retain a copy of DA Form 3078 and DA Form 4886 for IMA Soldiers. These forms will be maintained in accordance with AR 25–400–2.

(5) A completed copy of the DA Form 3078 or a current copy of DA Form 4886 will be sent to the Commander, HRC, (AHRC–ALL–S), 1600 Spearhead Division Avenue, Fort Knox, KY 40121–5205.

(6) After the wear out date on obsolete items has been achieved, the obsolete items will be replaced. This does not include optional items.

(7) The unit supply will dispose of all obsolete or damaged uniform items in accordance with established disposal procedures.

b. Lost items will be replaced by the Soldier.

14–17. Active Guard Reserve and Active Component Soldiers assigned to troop program units

a. Upon arrival of Active Guard Reserve (AGR) or active duty Soldiers to a USAR troop program unit (TPU) for permanent duty, the commander will direct an inspection and inventory of all personal clothing. Shortages of initial issue items will be requested within 15 days of assignment (see para 14–19c). Missing clothing items, other than initial issue shortages, will be replaced at the Soldier's expense within 30 days of assignment.

b. At the commander's discretion, corporals through sergeants major may furnish a statement, as shown in table 1-2, certifying they have all required clothing in accordance with CTA 50–900, and that all items meet the appearance standards of AR 670–1.

c. Enlisted AGR Soldiers begin accruing the CRA and are not authorized issue-in-kind replacement of personal clothing once they have completed six months (180 days) of their active duty tour and are receiving a CRA. Active duty or AGR Soldiers receiving a CRA must purchase replacement and new issue items of personal clothing.

14–18. Unauthorized alterations

Commanders will not permit unauthorized alterations to personal clothing. Authorized alterations are identified in tables 13–1 and 13–2. Replacement for items that have undergone unauthorized alterations, such as form fitting, pegging, or tapering will be replaced at the Soldier's expense.

14–19. Authorized alterations

USAR enlisted Soldiers in remote sites are authorized local alterations and will be reimbursed for the following alterations:

a. Alterations on uniforms issued from the CCDF will be completed locally using the Government purchase card.

b. Alterations on uniforms purchased at AMCS:

(1) The U.S. Army Soldier and Biological Chemical Command will request funds in the budget to cover the cost of DLA–TS ASUs alteration purchased at AMCS for USAR enlisted Soldiers in remote sites.

(2) Commanders will ensure enlisted Soldiers are measured and the measurements are annotated on the Soldier's DA Form 3078 and the form is sent to the Exchange.

c. USAR procedures for alteration of DLA–TS ASUs for USAR enlisted Soldiers in remote AMCS sites are as follows:

(1) AMCS prepares an alteration slip for each DA Form 3078 that includes the Soldier's name on each alteration slip. Alteration slips must be processed within 90 days.

(2) Commanders will send alteration slips to AMCS for reimbursement, as required.

(3) The AMCS will forward checks to the unit in each Soldier's name in an amount up to the authorized cost of alteration in paragraph 14–20c(2).

d. USAR local alterations at government expense or for reimbursement are limited to the following alterations:

(1) Coat sleeve hemming, cost $14.00.

(2) Trouser hemming, cost $8.00.

(3) Slack hemming, cost $8.00.

(4) Skirt hemming, cost 10.75.

(5) Waist alteration, $9.50.

(6) Seat alteration, $9.50.

(7) Any additional alterations required to make the uniform fit in accordance with AR 670–1, cost to be determined.

14–20. Clothing for Soldiers enrolled in the Reserve Officers' Training Corps Simultaneous Membership Program

a. Soldiers enrolled as officer trainees under the ROTC Simultaneous Membership Program according to AR 601–210 will be issued their personal and OCIE initial clothing allowances listed in CTA 50–900 in the same manner as other USAR Soldiers.

b. If personal clothing or OCIE issued to ROTC Simultaneous Membership Program Soldiers becomes lost, damaged, or destroyed, the USAR unit to which the ROTC Simultaneous Membership Program trainee is assigned will submit the appropriate adjustment document (DD Form 200 when an investigation is required), or DD Form 362 when liability is admitted, as required by this regulation and AR 735–5, through command channels to the appointing or approving authorities.

14–21. Exchange or replacement of personal clothing for U.S. Army Reserve troop program unit Soldiers

a. Exchange of personal clothing. This is authorized when—

(1) USAR TPU Soldiers complete a minimum of 3 years USAR service from date of initial clothing issue. For prior service Soldiers, initial clothing issue date is further defined as the date Soldier is brought up to full USAR clothing authorization. This establishes 3 years as the minimum usage criteria under which clothing exchanges will be authorized. This does not, however, constitute a blanket authorization to exchange all items of personal clothing simply because they are three or more years old.

(2) Items become unserviceable through FWT.

(3) Items are required because of size change (gain or loss of weight).

b. Replacement of personal clothing. This is authorized when—

(1) Items are lost, damaged or destroyed through no fault or negligence of the individual. A memorandum signed by the unit commander is required, per AR 735–5, in lieu of other adjustment documents.

(2) Items are destroyed by order of a medical officer. A statement signed by the medical officer or unit commander is required, per AR 735–5, in lieu of other adjustment documents.

(3) Items are lost, damaged or destroyed through fault or negligence of the individual and are adjusted by adjustment documents (DD Form 362), per AR 735–5.

c. Exchange of personal clothing items.

(1) When a Soldier notifies the unit they need an exchange of clothing, the unit supply sergeant will make a determination of serviceability, prior to making the recommendation for exchange and requesting the replacement items.

(2) Items that do not meet the minimum usage criteria will not be requisitioned without the signature of the unit commander.

(3) After the requested clothing items are received at the unit, the exchange of clothing will take place between the supply sergeant and the Soldier.

(4) Copies of CCDF Form 3078 or DA Form 3078 requesting clothing exchanges are filed in the Soldier's personal clothing record file and serve as an indicator to determine and prevent excess clothing exchanges.

(5) Unit supply sergeants or specialists prepare DA Form 3078 in accordance with paragraph 1–6p.

d. Replacement of personal clothing items.

(1) The unit supply sergeant will complete DA Form 3078 per paragraph 14–14 and check "Replacement" in Block 12.

(2) Clothing replacement requires a statement justifying the transaction in all cases. The statement can be included on the DA Form 3078 or be in the form of an attached memorandum or statement signed by the unit commander or medical officer. Adjustment documents in accordance with AR 735–5, to include document numbers, may also be attached

Chapter 15
Clothing Support to the Army National Guard

Section I
Army National Guard Central Clothing Distribution Facility

15–1. Establishment
The DLA–TS has established a contractor-operated CCDF to serve ARNG customers.

15–2. Mission
The mission of the CCDF is to provide ARNG enlisted Soldiers authorized issue-in-kind with their total requirements for military clothing, including insignia and decorations, from a single location. Ordering is available at http://www.kyloc.com, with other options for units lacking internet access. Requests for CCDF Web site access are processed through the appropriate USPFO or DOL. Orders are configured and shipped directly to units in Soldier kits with name and Army tapes affixed, as applicable.

15–3. Inventories
a. The CCDF inventory of new material is owned by DLA–TS. States are billed monthly for issues to their units during the previous month. The billing and billing validation processes are described in the CCD management plan.

b. The CCDF inventory of used, recyclable garments is owned by the NGB. Recycling is centrally funded by NGB and issues to unit are made on a free issue basis.

15–4. Sale of clothing by the central clothing distribution facility
Only individuals authorized issue-in-kind are supported by the CCDF. The CCDF will not make cash or credit sales. Individuals needing to purchase clothing will use AMCS facilities or Exchange Internet or mail order sales options (see chap 12).

Section II
Issue-in-Kind for Army National Guard Personal Clothing

15–5. Introduction
a. The issue-in-kind system will be used by ARNG in the replacement of personal clothing.

b. Entitlements to initial allowances are discussed in chapter 4.

c. The retention and disposition of clothing is discussed in chapter 12.

d. Alterations will be made at Government expense under the provisions of chapter 13.

e. ARNG requirements for personal clothing are provided by a CCDF operated by a DLA–TS contractor. Policy and procedures for operation of the CCD system are established by NGB and disseminated to States in a CCD Management Plan and to units in a CCD User Handbook. States tailor the User Handbook to their unique requirements by insertion of State policies into its appendix D and distribute the handbook to the unit level.

f. Each state appoints a CCD State Administrator who is responsible to the USPFO or the Director of Logistics for administration of the CCD Program within the State.

g. Requests for personal clothing are submitted directly from the customer unit to the CCDF via the Internet, using the CCDF Web site at http://www.ngmmc.com or http://www.ngmmc.ngb.army.mil. Requests are submitted on the online electronic forms using the electronic CCDF Form 3078–1 (preferred ordering medium). Units lacking internet access can order by facsimile, email, telephone, or U.S. Mail. Toll Free Numbers are 1–888–255–1131, Fax 1–888–356–2443 or using Web site http://www.kyloc.com. Issues by the CCDF are documented on the CCDF Form 3078–1 that accompanies each shipment.

h. Personal clothing will be accounted for on DA Form 4886. Samples of a completed DA Form 4886 and completion instructions are contained in figure 14–1. Overprinting of this form is authorized. The unit commander's representative may acknowledge turn-ins.

i. ARNG Soldiers receiving a CRA are not authorized support using the issue-in-kind or the CCDF. This includes all ARNG Soldiers on active duty in excess of 179 days.

j. Unit commanders will establish an expendable or durable document register for personal clothing not available through the CCDF. Completed document register pages will be filed per AR 25–400–2. The last name of the individual for whom the clothing is ordered will be shown in column N, "Remarks" of the document register.

15–6. Requests for personal clothing
a. To receive support from the CCDF, the following three actions must be completed.

(1) The unit's Department of Defense Activity Address Code must be registered with the CCDF by the CCD State Administrator or a designee.

(2) A user identification and password by the CCD State Administrator or a designee must be allocated.

(3) Be allocated ordering authority by the CCD State Administrator or their designee.

b. The ordering process employed by units is described in detail in the CCD User Handbook. Units with Internet access will order via the Internet.

c. Most orders will be processed for a single Soldier. All items required for a single Soldier can be ordered on a single order and will be shipped as a Soldier kit.

d. The CCDF ordering system will also accept bulk orders from any Department of Defense activities address code or unit authorized to order from the CCDF. The CCDF will issue no more than 35 shoulder sleeve insignias, and no more than 10 of each of any other items on a single bulk order.

e. Federal awards, decorations, and insignia are available for requisition from the CCDF. States are encouraged to make and disseminate policy restricting bulk orders.

f. Requests for special measurement clothing or footwear will be processed as outlined in chapter 5 of the CCD User Handbook.

g. ARNG units are authorized to establish an on-shelf inventory of rank and organization shoulder insignia. Inventory is not to exceed 5 sets of rank insignia per enlisted grade, subdued and brass, and 25 of each applicable type of shoulder sleeve insignia. Other personal clothing items may be stocked if specifically permitted by State policy found in appendix D of the CCD User Handbook.

h. Disposition of CCDF Form 3078–1 will be as follows:

(1) The original copy will be posted to the appropriate DA Form 4886 and filed in the individual's clothing file.

(2) The CCDF Form 3078–1 will be destroyed after review by the Command Supply Discipline Program inspection team.

15–7. Army National Guard personnel attending annual training, Army area school, or Army service schools other than initial activity duty for training

a. Unit commanders are required to ensure that ARNG personnel are equipped with all required personal clothing from ARNG stocks prior to departure for attendance at annual training, National Training Center, Joint Readiness Training Center, overseas deployment training, Army area school, or Army service school.

b. The season, location of the school, duration of the training, and the nature and type of schooling or training will determine the type and quantity of clothing to be taken to or issued at the school or installation. Prior coordination by the State Adjutant General with the commandant of the school is required to ascertain specifics or special clothing requirements. Such coordination will ensure that required clothing will accompany the individual or be available for issue at the school.

c. When the ASU is prescribed for wear in the classroom in excess of 30 days, the school commandant, with State Adjutant General approval, may issue one additional uniform shirt as authorized by CTA 50–900. The extra uniform shirt will be turned in upon return from the school.

d. When ARNG enlisted personnel arrive at annual training, or Army area schools or Army service schools without adequate individual clothing, installation commanders are authorized to issue required items or replace unserviceable items from AMCS on a case by case basis, in accordance with the following procedures:

(1) The unit supply sergeant or specialist of the student's company or detachment will prepare a DA Form 3078.

(2) The unit supply sergeant or specialist of the student's company or detachment will provide the AMCS five copies of DA Form 3078, completed according to the example in figure 3–1, with two copies of the Soldier's orders.

(3) All ARNG personnel will present their identification, the five copies of the DA Form 3078, and two copies of their orders reflecting the accounting classification to be charged at the AMCS.

(4) It is the commander's responsibility to ensure that issues made under the provisions of paragraph 15–7*d*(1) be properly posted to the Soldier's DA Form 4886.

(5) DA Form 4886 and DA Form 3645, accompanying the student or forwarded to the school by other means, will be returned to the National Guard unit to which the Soldier is assigned.

(6) The USPFO will reimburse items of an Army area school or Army service school that requires ARNG students or cadets to have or additional quantities of items not authorized to the ARNG.

(7) Clothing and equipment above school requirements and in the possession of the student upon reporting to the school will not be withdrawn by the school or installation. Replacement of excess items that become unserviceable is not authorized. Unserviceable excess items will be turned into the USPFO.

e. It is mandatory that special measurement clothing and footwear be requisitioned by the USPFO for issue to ARNG enlisted personnel prior to departure for an Army area school or Army service school. Such items are not stocked at Army installations.

15–8. Accounting for personal clothing

a. All personal clothing issued to individuals in the ARNG will be accounted for on DA Form 4886.

b. Unit commanders will ensure that Soldiers have in their possession at all times and in a serviceable condition, those items posted to their clothing records. Commanders will conduct inspections of personal clothing annually to ensure that all items are on hand and serviceable. The date of the last inspection will be recorded in the remarks block. Write "per inspection" or "per insp" and sign and date and initial in pencil. Items lost, damaged, or destroyed through neglect or other than indicated in paragraph 15–9 will be adjusted per AR 735–5. Commanders may permit corporals through sergeants major to furnish a statement in lieu of inspection that they have all their clothing and that items are serviceable.

c. The following actions are taken when a new DA Form 4886 is required:

(1) The previous balances are posted in ink on the new form in the first column. The unused blocks in the column are ruled out in ink. The signature of the individual, along with the date, is placed at the bottom of the column. The old DA Form 4886 is retained with the individual's personal clothing record until the next CSDP review.

(2) If DA Form 4886 is lost, the unit commander directs that an inventory of personal clothing be executed. Quantities of items in laundries or repair shops are inventoried as on hand. Based on this inventory, a new DA Form 4886 is prepared. The new form is annotated in the name block, "Replaces lost form." Quantities on hand within authorized allowances are placed in column 1. Items less than the allowance are replaced at the Soldier's expense, unless the Soldier proves that the items were never issued.

d. To track the frequency of exchanges, supply sergeants will record on the ARNG Soldier's DA Form 4886 exchanges or replacements which do not result in a change in the quantity of an item in the Soldier's possession. The following actions are required:

(1) Insert, in pencil, in the available blank space in the "Personal Clothing Items" column for the affected item, the

Julian date of the exchange and, in parentheses, the quantity exchanged. (Example: "0200 (1)" would denote an exchange of one item on 18 July 2000).

(2) Maintain a maximum of three exchange records for each type of item. When a fourth exchange takes place, erase the oldest record, and replace it with the current record.

15–9. Accounting for personal clothing on change of status

a. When the assignment or duty station of an enlisted Soldier changes within or between States, ARNG units, or the USAR, the personal clothing record will be transferred to the gaining organization. All personal clothing items (does not include OCIE) will remain in the possession of the enlisted Soldier.

b. Individuals discharged from the ARNG will return personal clothing upon separation, as prescribed by table 12–1 and by the CCD User Handbook. DA Form 4886 will be adjusted to show clothing items retained and will be filed in the individual's unit file.

c. Individuals transferring from traditional ARNG to AGR status will retain all personal clothing.

d. Individuals discharged from the Active Army and enlisting in the ARNG within 90 days, will report to their unit with all personal clothing items per paragraph 12–1e and the personal clothing receipt statement referred to in paragraph 12–10. Persons reporting to their unit without the personal clothing receipt statement referred to in paragraph 12–10 are required to adjust for the missing clothing (see AR 735–5).

e. Individuals who have completed their obligation will have their DA Form 4886 filed in their unit file. If the individual returns to the ARNG within 1 year, items retained will be inventoried and checked for serviceability between the individual and unit supply personnel. Missing items of personal clothing are replaced at the individual's expense.

15–10. Turn-ins

a. Serviceable turn-ins of clothing that is cost effectively recyclable will be made as prescribed in the CCD User Handbook. States may establish in-State recycling programs for other garments if such programs comply with NGB guidance found in the CCD Management Plan. Other items of clothing turned-in by Soldiers will be processed as prescribed by the CCD User Handbook.

b. All turn-ins will be documented on CCDF Form 3161 or CCDF Form 3161M. One copy of the form will be retained in the Soldier's clothing record.

c. Turn-ins of used or obsolete new items of clothing that are not cost-effectively recyclable will be marked as prescribed in the CCD User Handbook and returned to the Soldier for disposition. Unserviceable clothing will receive a FWT determination by an Active Army or ARNG officer as prescribed in paragraph 12–1 of this regulation and in 32 USC 710(f).

d. Items determined to be unserviceable for reasons of other than FWT will be accounted for by an appropriate adjustment action under the provisions of AR 735–5.

15–11. Exchange or replacement of personal clothing

a. Exchange of personal clothing is authorized when—
(1) ARNG members complete a minimum of 3 years of National Guard service. This is established as the minimum usage criteria under which clothing exchanges will be authorized.
(2) Items become unserviceable through FWT.
(3) Items are needed because of size change.

b. Replacement of personal clothing is authorized when—
(1) Items are destroyed or lost through no fault of the individual.
(2) Items are destroyed by order of a medical officer.
(3) Accountable records for items are adjusted in accordance with AR 735–5.

c. The following method will be used to exchange clothing. The individual notifies the unit of the need to exchange clothing and presents the garment to validate the need. A request for clothing is submitted to the CCDF. After the requested clothing is received at the unit, the exchange of clothing will take place between the unit representative and the individual. DA Form 4886 will not be adjusted if a single item is exchanged or if the request for exchange of multiple items is filled by the CCDF at the same time. Pencil notation of the exchange is posted to the Soldier's DA Form 4886 as prescribed by paragraph 15–8d and by the CCD User Handbook. This serves as a tool to prevent excessive exchange of unserviceable clothing. Requests are submitted per paragraph 15–6 and turn-ins are made per paragraph 15–10. The unit representative will select "Exchange" on the CCDF issue request used to request clothing in an exchange transaction.

d. Replacement of clothing will be accomplished by completing a CCDF issue request in accordance with the CCD User Handbook. The unit representative will select "Replacement" to request clothing in a replacement transaction.

e. The CCDF will recycle those types of personal clothing that can be cost effectively recycled and meet serviceability standards established by the NGB. The cost of recycling will be centrally funded and issues will be made without charge to the requestor.

15–12. Optional exchange procedures for personal clothing

a. The following optional method may be used to exchange unserviceable clothing. This process is used primarily when an ARNG or active officer is not expected to be able to be present to make a FWT determination at the time replacement clothing will be issued to the Soldier. The Soldier turns in personal clothing items requiring replacement to the unit representative. The unit representative will prepare DA Form 2402 (Maintenance Tag) or CCDF Form 3161 as prescribed by the CCD User Handbook. The clothing will be held at the unit level pending completion of the FWT determination by an ARNG or Active Army officer.

b. Upon receipt of the replacement items from the CCDF, the unit representative issues them to the Soldier and adjusts the Soldier's DA Form 4886 to reflect the issue.

Chapter 16
Evaluations and Inspections

16–1. Deputy Chief of Staff, G–4
The DCS, G–4 will establish internal controls to provide reasonable assurance that obligations and cost are in compliance with applicable laws; funds, property, and other assets are safeguarded against waste, loss or unauthorized use, or misappropriation of revenues and expenditures are properly recorded and accounted for.

16–2. Evaluations
Headquarters, TACOM, CSO is the authorized agent responsible for the conduction of evaluations of The Exchange operated AMCS.

a. Installation commanders (garrison) and exchange general managers will provide administrative and technical assistance as requested by the CSO to assist in the evaluation.

b. The CSO will furnish an annual evaluation report through the Exchange HQ for the general managers and the evaluated facility. The evaluation report contains the CSO's findings and recommendations. The CSO will continue to monitor and follow-up on incomplete actions related to the evaluation.

c. The CSO will use professional judgment and explicitly identify the key internal controls essential to the operation of the AMCS.

d. The CSO will develop an internal control evaluation and publish it as an appendix in this regulation to be used by managers in evaluating key internal controls.

16–3. Internal controls

a. Formally designed procedures – annual inventories and reconciliations.

b. Checks and balances – limitation of access.

c. Recurring reports, internal reviews, supervisory monitoring and performance reviews.

d. Physical devices – secured installations, facilities, storages, files, and safes.

e. Key internal controls are absolutely essential for ensuring that processes operates as intended and resources are safeguarded from fraud, waste, and misuse.

16–4. Purpose
This regulation provides the following internal controls which directly relates to GAO standards for internal controls.

a. Communicate guidance.

b. Contribute to good management of government resources and human capital.

c. The controls of this regulation will not exceed benefits derived, however a certain amount of risk is accepted.

Appendix A
References

Section I
Required Publications

AR 12–15
Joint Security Cooperation Education and Training (Cited in para 3–1h.)

AR 32–4
Special Measurement Clothing and Footwear, Orthopedic Footwear, Guidons, Streamers, and Flags (Cited in paras 7–2a, 7–4a, and 7–6.)

AR 145–1
Senior Reserve Officers' Training Corps Program: Organization, Administration, and Training (Cited in paras 9–2b, 9–2c, 10–5b, 10–7a, 10–7c(1), 10–7c(2), 10–7c(2), 10–7c(3), and 10–7c(4).)

AR 190–30
Military Police Investigations (Cited in para 8–3b.)

AR 210–20
Real Property Master Planning for Army Installations (Cited in para1-4e(6).)

AR 638–2
Care and Disposition of Remains and Disposition of Personal Effects (Cited in paras 12–17, 12–19.)

AR 670–1
Wear and Appearance of Army Uniforms and Insignia (Cited in paras 1–4, 1–7, 3–1, 3–3k(2), 5–5, 11–4, 14–18, and 14–20.)

AR 710–2
Supply Policy Below the National Level (Cited in paras 2–7, 5–6, 9–9, 9–10, and 10–6.)

AR 725–50
Requisition, Receipt, and Issue System. (Cited in paras 7–2, 9–5.)

AR 735–5
Property Accountability Policies (Cited in 9–11b; 9–13d and e; table 12–1; table 12–6; 12–14e; 14–5e; 14–6b(2); 14–8b(3) and (5); 14–10b; 14–11a; 14–15e; 14–18b; 14–19b(1), (2), and (3) and d(12); 15–8b; 15–9d; 15–10d; and 15–11a(b)(3).)

CTA 50–900
Clothing and Individual Equipment (Cited in paras 1–4i(1); 2–7b; 4–1; 4–2d(2) and e; 4–6a; 4–7; 4–8d and e; 4–9a; 5–4f; 5–6a; 5–7a; 5–12b; 6–1b; 9–1a and d; 9–3c; 9–10c; 12–5a; 14–5e; 14–9a; 14–12a(3); 14–13a; 14–15b; 14–18a; 15–7c; and 15–9c.) (Available at https://webtaads.belvoir.army.mil/USAFMSA.)

DA Pam 25–403
Guide to Recordkeeping in the Army (Cited in para 14–6.)

DA Pam 638–2
Procedures for the Care and Disposition of Remains and Disposition of Personal Effects (Cited in para 5-4b.)

DA Pam 710–2–1
Using Unit Supply System (Manual Procedures) (Cited in paras 1–7n, 4–9b, 6–6b(2), 9–10b, 10–6, and 12–16*c*.)

DODD 4500.54E
Department of Defense Foreign Clearance Guide (Cited in paras 8–2a(4) and 8–2b(1).)

DODI 1338.18
Armed Forces Clothing Monetary Allowance Procedures (Cited in para 8–1a.)

SB 10–523
Size Tariff for Clothing, Equipage and Footwear (Cited in para 14–1d.)

TM 10–227
Fitting of Army Uniforms and Footwear (Cited in paras 1–7d, 6–1b, 6–6d, 6–7h, 14–1d, and table 13–1.)

TM 10–8400–201–23
Unit and Direct Support Maintenance Manual for General Repair Procedures for Clothing (Cited in para 1–7m.)

Section II
Related Publications
A related publication is a source of additional information. The user does not have to read it to understand the regulation. USCs are available at http://www.access.gpo.gov/index.html.

AR 1–75
Administrative and Logistical Support of Overseas Security Assistance Organizations (SAOS)

AR 11–2
Manager's Internal Control Program

AR 25–30
The Army Publishing Program

AR 25–400–2
The Army Records Information Management System (ARIMS)

AR 27–20
Claims

AR 40–3
Medical, Dental, and Veterinary Care

AR 135–91
Service Obligations, Method of Fulfillment, Participation Requirements, and Enforcement Procedures

AR 135–178
Enlisted Administrative Separations

AR 140–10
Assignments, Attachments, Details, and Transfers

AR 210–130
Laundry and Dry Cleaning Operations

AR 600–8–22
Military Awards

AR 600–9
The Army Body Composition Program

AR 601–210
Active and Reserve Components Enlistment Program

AR 635–200
Active Duty Enlisted Administrative Separations

AR 640–30
Photographs for Military Human Resources Records

AR 930–5
American National Red Cross Service Program and Army Utilization

Central Clothing Distribution User Handbook
(Available at the Kentucky Logistics Operations Center, 5751 Briar Hill Rd., Bldg. 6, Lexington, KY 40516–9721).

DA Pam 600–8
Management and Administrative Procedures

DA Pam 710–2–1
Using Unit Supply System (Manual Procedures)

DOD 4500.9–R
Department of Defense Transportation Regulation (Available at http://www.dtic.mil/whs/directives/corres/htm/45009r.htm).

DODI 1325.07
Administration of Military Correctional Facilities and Clemency and Parole Authority

EO 10113
Delegating the Authority of the President to Prescribe Clothing Allowances, and Cash Allowances in Lieu Thereof, for Enlisted Men in the Armed Forces (Available at http://www.archives.gov/federal_register/executive_orders/disposition_tables.html.)

EOP 40–4
Military Clothing Sales Stores (Available at https://www.us.army.mil/suite/page/633544).

TM 10–227
Fitting of Army Uniforms and Footwear (Available at http://www.logsa.army.mil.)

SB 700 (FEDLOG)
Army Adopted/Other Items Selected for Authorization/List of Reportable Items (Available at http://weblog.logsa.army.mil/index.shtml.)

UCMJ
Uniform Code of Military Justice (Available at http://www.army.mil/references/ucmj.)

5 USC 5901
Uniform allowances

10 USC 771
Department of the Army: Seal

10 USC 4562
Clothing

10 USC 4621
Quartermaster supplies: members of armed services; veterans; executive or military departments and employees; prices

10 USC 772
When wearing by persons not on active duty authorized

32 USC 710(f)
Accountability for Property Issued to the National Guard

37 USC 418
Clothing allowance: enlisted members

37 USC 419
Civilian clothing allowance

Section III
Prescribed Forms

Unless otherwise indicated, DA Forms are available on the APD Web site (http://www.apd.army.mil) and DD Forms are available on the OSD Web site (http://www.dtic.mil/whs/directives/infomgt/forms/).

DA Form 3078
Personal Clothing Request (Prescribed in throughout the publication.)

DA Form 4886
Issue-In-Kind Personal Clothing Record (Prescribed in chaps 1, 5, 12 and 14.)

DA Form 7000
Delegation of Authority - Army Military Clothing Stores (Prescribed in paras 1–7, 5–2, 5–6, and 14–2.)

DD Form 754
Repair Tag (Prescribed in para 6–8.) (Available through normal forms supply channels.)

Section IV
Referenced Forms

Unless otherwise indicated, DA Forms are available on the APD Web site (http://www.apd.army.mil) and DD Forms are available on the OSD Web site (http://www.dtic.mil/whs/directives/infomgt/forms/). SFs are available on the General Services Administration Web site (http://www.gsa.gov/portal/forms/type/SF).

CCDF Form 2
Request for Access Form

CCDF Form 3
Personal Clothing Request

CCDF Form 3078
(CCDF Mail or FAX Request) New Garments)

CCDF Form 3078–1
Personal Clothing Request (Available at http://www.ngmmc.com.)

CCDF Form 3078–2
(CCDF Mail or FAX Request) Recycled Garments)

CCDF Form 3161
Request for Turn-In (Available at http://www.ngmmc.com.)

CCDF Form 3161M
Request for Turn-In Manual (Available at http://www.ngmmc.com.)

DA Form 11–2
Internal Control Evaluation Certification

DA Form 137–2
Installation Clearance Record

DA Form 1687
Notice of Delegation of Authority-Receipt for Supplies

DA Form 2028
Recommended Changes to Publications and Blank Forms

DA Form 2062
Hand Receipt/Annex Number

DA Form 2402
Maintenance Tag (Available through normal forms supply channels.)

DA Form 2765–1
Request for Issue or Turn-In

DA Form 3645
Organizational Clothing and Individual Equipment Record

DA Form 3645–1
Additional Organizational Clothing and Individual Equipment Record

DA Form 4949
Administrative Adjustment Report (AAR)

DA Form 5965
Basis of Issue for Clothing and Individual Equipment (CIE)

DD Form 139
Pay Adjustment Authorization

DD Form 150
Special Measurements Blank for Special Measurements/Orthopedic Boots and Shoes

DD Form 200
Financial Liability Investigation of Property Loss

DD Form 214
Certificate of Release or Discharge from Active Duty (Available through normal forms supply channels.)

DD Form 358
Armed Forces Measurement Blank-Special Sized Clothing for Men

DD Form 361
Transportation Discrepancy Report (TDR)

DD Form 362
Statement of Charges/Cash Collection Voucher

DD Form 1111
Armed Forces Measurement Blank-Special Sized Clothing for Women.

DD Form 1173
Uniformed Services Identification and Privilege Card (Available through normal forms supply channels.)

DD Form 1348
DOD Single Line Item Requisition System Document (Manual)

DD Form 1348–1A
Issue Release/Receipt Document

DD Form 1348–6
DOD Single Line Item Requisition System Document (Manual-Long Form)

SF 364
Report of Discrepancy (ROD)

SF 368
Product Quality Deficiency Report (PQDR)

SF 1034
Public Voucher for Purchases and Services Other Than Personal

Appendix B
Internal Control Evaluation

B–1. Function
The function of the process is to evaluate efficiency and effectiveness of the issue and sale of personal clothing.

B–2. Purpose
The purpose of this evaluation is to assist users in evaluating their key management controls. It is not intended to cover all controls. Key internal controls are absolutely essential for ensuring that processes operates as intended and resources are safeguarded from fraud, waste and misuse.

B–3. Instructions
Answers must be based on the actual testing of key internal controls such as document analysis, direct observation, interviewing, sampling, and simulation. Answers that indicate deficiencies must be explained and corrective action indicated in supporting documentation. These management controls must be evaluated at least once every 5 years. Certification that the evaluation has been conducted must be accomplished on DA Form 11–2 (Internal Control Evaluation Certification).

B–4. Test questions
   a. Military clothing general information and/or overall appearance.
   (1) Are the clothing displays neat and attractive (see this regulation)?
   (2) Are dressing rooms accessible and serviceable (doors close, mirror, and chair) (see this regulation)?
   (3) Are sizes and prices clearly displayed (see this regulation)?
   (4) Are garments displayed on mannequins/forms properly fitted (see this regulation), dust free, and conform to AR 670–1?
   b. Review documentation and/or DA Form 3078.
   (1) Are enlisted Soldiers receiving alterations, for DLA–TS items, at no cost (enlisted only)?
   (2) A review of alteration certificates for compliance (see EOP 40–4, 8–27).
   (3) Are alteration shop personnel separating DLA–TS from Exchange alteration certificates before logging them into the alteration certificates, and the Alteration Shop Control Sheet (see EOP 40–4, 8-27)?
   c. Alterations.
   (1) Are enlisted Soldiers receiving alterations, for DLA–TS items, at no cost (enlisted only)?
   (2) A review of alteration certificates for compliance (see EOP 40–4, 8–27).
   (3) Are alteration shop personnel separating DLA–TS from Exchange alteration certificates before logging them into the alteration certicicates, and the Alteration Shop Control Sheet (see EOP 40–4, 8–27)?
   d. Supply management.
   (1) Are PQDR for defective merchandise received by the Exchange Military Clothing being reported to the CSO (see this regulation)?
   (2) Were the PQDR submitted within 30 days after identifying the quality deficiency (see AR 700–84)?
   (3) Is the merchandise for all PQDRs being held until receipt of disposition instructions and is all merchandise properly identified to reconcile with the PQDR document (see AR 700–84)?
   (4) Has the Exchange manager received disposition instructions for PQDRs and disposed of the merchandise as prescribed by the disposition instructions (see AR 700–84)?
   (5) Are request for SDR being submitted by exchange to CSO within 45 days (see EOP 40–4)?
   (6) Has DD Form 1348–1A (Issue Release/Receipt Document) been reviewed and discrepancies noted (see EOP 40–4)?
   (7) Has the Exchange submitted request for FTE to the CSO for disposition (see EOP 40–4)?
   (8) After reviewing requisition documents, is the AMCS ordering process in compliance with Exchange directive of requisitioning weekly (see EOP 40–4)?
   e. Merchandising.
   (1) Are Condition Code "B" clothing items being received (see this regulation)?
   (2) Are the Condition Code "B" clothing items displayed separately from the new clothing items (see this regulation)?

(3) Are the Condition Code "B" clothing items clearly marked and identified with correct pricing (50 percent off the federal regulated price) (see this regulation)?

(4) Are the Condition Code "B" clothing items being depreciated after 60/90 days and credited to the 109–12 account (see this regulation)?

(5) Are the Condition Code "B" standards being enforced when exchanges are made at the Clothing Sales Store (see this regulation)?

(6) Are there any optional or non-uniform item displays distracting the view of DLA–TS items (see EOP 40–4)?

(7) Does the AMCS transfer DLA–TS merchandise in accordance with EOP 40–4?

(8) Is there an exception to policy on file for transfers to nonappropriated facilities (see EOP 40–4)?

f. Organizational clothing and individual equipment.

(1) Is the AMCS manager aware of the policy outlined in the MOA between HQDA and HQ AAFES on stocking OCIE items (see MOA)?

(2) Was there an attempt to contact the CIF to verify list with their inventory (see this regulation)?

(3) Does the CIF maintain stockage of items currently on stock at AMCS (see this regulation and EOP 40–4)?

(4) Is there an approved letter on file and up-to-date for the items of OCIE stocked (see this regulation and MOA)?

(5) Do the items on the shelf match the letter (see this regulation and MOA)?

(6) Are there expendable items or MOS specific OCIE on sale (see this regulation)?

B–5. Supersession
This evaluation replaces the evaluation previously published in AR 700–84, dated 15 June 2010.

B–6. Comment
Help make this a better tool for the issue and sale of personal clothing submit comments to the Deputy Chief of Staff, G–4 (DALO–SUI), 500 Army Pentagon, Washington, DC 20310–0500.

Glossary

Section I
Abbreviations

ACOM
Army command

ACU
Army combat uniform

ADO
Army direct ordering

ADSW
active duty for special work

AGR
Active Duty Guard/Reserve

AMC
U.S. Army Materiel Command

AMCS
Army military clothing store

ARNG
Army National Guard

ASA (ALT)
Assistant Secretary of the Army (Acquisitions, Logistics and Technology)

ASCC
Army service component command

ASU
Army service uniform

CB
clothing bag

CCA
civilian-clothing allowance

CCD
central clothing distribution

CCDF
central clothing distribution facility

CENTCOM
U.S. Central Command

CEO
chief executive officer

CIDC
U.S. Army Criminal Investigation Command

CIF
central issue facility

CIIP
clothing initial issue point

CMA
clothing monetary allowance

CNGB
Chief, National Guard Bureau

COAD
continued on active duty

COAR
continued on Active Reserve

CONUS
continental United States

CRA
clothing replacement allowance

CSO
Clothing and Services Office

CTA
common table of allowance

DA
Department of the Army

DA Pam
Department of the Army pamphlet

DCS, G–1
Deputy Chief of Staff, G–1

DCS, G–4
Deputy Chief of Staff, G–4

DEERS
Defense Enrollment Eligibility Reporting System

DFAS
Defense Finance and Accounting Service

DJMS
Defense Joint Military Pay System

DJMS–RC
Defense Joint Military Pay System–Reserve Component

DLA
Defense Logistics Agency

DLA–TS
Defense Logistics Agency–Troop Support

DOD
Department of Defense

DOD EMALL
Department of Defense electronic mall

DRCS
director of reserve component support

DRMS
Defense Reutilization and Marketing Service

DRU
director reporting unit

EOP
exchange operating procedures

EUCOM
U.S. European Command

EUSA
Eighth U.S. Army

FORSCOM
U.S. Army Forces Command

FWT
fair wear and tear

GSA
General Services Administration

HQDA
Headquarters, Department of the Army

HRC
U.S. Army Human Resources Command

IADT
initial active duty for training

IET
initial entry training

IMA
individual mobilization augmentation

INSCOM
U.S. Army Intelligence and Security Command

IPERMS
Interactive Personnel Electronic Records Management System

IRR
Individual Ready Reserve

ISD
installation supply division

JROTC
Junior Reserve Officer Training Corps

MAAG
Military Assistance Advisory Group

MC
military colleges

MDW
U.S. Army Military District of Washington

MEDCOM
U.S. Army Medical Command

MJC
military junior colleges

MOA
memorandum of agreement

MOS
military occupational specialty

MPA
military personnel, Army

MPC
military property custodian

MPI
military police investigator

MPS
military property specialist

MS
military science

NGB
National Guard Bureau

NGR
National Guard regulation

OCIE
organizational clothing and individual equipment

OCONUS
outside continental United States

OMA
Operation Maintenance, Army

OSD
Office of the Secretary of Defense

PBO
property book officer

PCF
personnel control facility

PMS
professor of military science

RC
Reserve Component

REFRAD
release from active duty

ROTC
Reserve Officers' Training Corps

RPA
reserve personnel, Army

SADT
special active duty for training

SB
supply bulletin

SDDC
Surface Deployment and Distribution Command

SF
standard form

SHAPE
Supreme Headquarters Allied Powers, Europe

SROTC
Army Senior Reserve Officers' Training Corps

SSN
social security number

TDY
temporary duty

TM
technical manual

TPU
troop program unit

TRADOC
U.S. Army Training and Doctrine Command

TWI
training with industry program

UCDPP
uniform clothing deferred payment plan

UCMJ
Uniform Code of Military Justice

USACC
U.S. Army Cadet Command

USACIDC
U.S. Army Criminal Investigation Command

USAR
U.S. Army Reserve

USPACOM
U.S. Pacific Command

USACE
U.S. Army Corps of Engineers

USAE
U.S. Army Element

USAISC
U.S. Army Information Systems Command

USARC
U.S. Army Reserve Command

USAREUR
U.S. Army Europe

USARPAC
U.S. Army Pacific

USASOC
U.S. Army Special Operations Command

USC
United States Code

USDB
U.S. Disciplinary Barracks

USPFO
U.S. Property and Fiscal Office

USSS
U.S. Secret Service

WTU
Warrior Transition Unit

WW
Wounded Warrior

WWCSP
Wounded Warrior Clothing Support Program

Section II
Terms

Active Duty Guard and/or Reserve Program
Program under which members of RCs can be accepted and voluntarily ordered to full-time active duty for periods of 180 days or more. These members provide full-time support to the Reserve Components and are paid from an ARNG or USAR personnel appropriation of a DOD military Service.

Army Military Clothing Store
A designated facility where Army uniforms, components, and insignia items are kept for sale or issue to authorized persons.

Army Military Clothing Store manager
A person designated by the local exchange manager to be responsible for AMCS supervision and AMCS operation. This definition does not include the Berlin clothing store or contractor-operated stores.

Central clothing distribution
A process involving the supplying of ARNG requirements for issue-in-kind personal clothing, insignia and decorations from a single distribution facility. Items are ordered by units directly from the distribution facility and shipped directly from the facility to units as Soldier kits.

Central clothing distribution facility
A distribution center operated by a DLA–TS contractor that receives orders for personal clothing, insignia and awards directly from units, customize uniforms by affixing specified insignia and ships by small parcel carrier to the requesting unit.

Central clothing distribution facility
A distribution center operated by a DLA–TS contractor that receives orders for personal clothing, insignia and awards directly from units, customize uniforms by affixing specified insignia and ships by small parcel carrier to the requesting unit.

Clothing Initial Issue Point
A facility normally located at an installation that serves as a reception station for new Soldiers being processed for training in the Active Army.

Clothing Issue Point
The facility which supports the WW with select CB items and select OCIE.

Clothing issue-in-kind
An alternate system for furnishing items or initial clothing and replacements at Government expense. Replacement is done by exchange of unserviceable garments for serviceable garments.

Clothing maintenance
Alteration and replacement by purchase of personal uniform clothing by the individual.

Clothing monetary allowance system
A system for furnishing the individual Soldier initial clothing allowance on an item basis.

Clothing replacement allowance
Funds allocated to Soldiers annually for replacement by purchase of personal uniform clothing by the individual.

Commutation in lieu of issue-in-kind
Monetary payment by the Government in lieu of issue-in-kind.

Continuous active duty or continuously on active duty
An interim of 3 months or less between date of discharge or release from active duty and date of reenlistment or recall to active duty.

Department of Defense – electronic mail
DOD EMALL is a comprehensive Web site providing access to over 22 million items for purchase to the DOD, federal, state and local governments.

Exchange
A Joint command of the U.S. Army and the U.S. Air Force under the jurisdiction of the Chief of Staff, U.S. Army and the Chief of Staff, U.S. Air Force that furnishes activities, personnel, property, and nonappropriated funds through which exchange and motion picture services are provided.

Extended active duty
A period of active duty exceeding 6 months

Fair wear and tear
Loss or impairment of appearance, effectiveness, worth, or utility of an item that has occurred solely because of normal and customary use of the item for its intended purpose.

Full-time support personnel
Those who assist in training, administration, maintenance, and operation of ARNG units and perform a variety of functions relative to the management of the ARNG.

Gratuitous issue
An issue or replacement of personal clothing, not in excess of authorized allowances, without cost to an enlisted person.

Initial clothing allowance
Prescribed items and quantities of personal type clothing and service uniforms, with component items, furnished to enlisted members when entitled to an initial issue of clothing allowance.

Inventory
An inventory is a physical count of property on hand.

Military property custodian
Agent of a school who maintains accountability and responsibility for Army property. He or she is authorized to requisition, receive, store, issue, account for, and perform administrative functions require in connection with using Government property furnished the institution by the Army or the Air Force, or both, in connection with ROTC training. The agent may be military or civilian.

Military property specialist
A bonded agent of a school who is authorized to requisition, receive, store, issue and account for property, and perform administrative functions connected with the use of Government property provided to the school by the DA for Junior ROTC training.

Nonprior service
Nonprior service for persons enlisting in USAR; never served or have served less than 180 days of Active Duty and are not MOS qualified.

Nonrecoverable items
Personal clothing items of enlisted members not to be turned in or accounted for on termination of service. Nonrecoverable personal clothing items are headgear, belts, boots, buckles, underwear, necklace, necktabs, neckties, gloves, handbags, towels, scarves, handkerchiefs, shoes, socks, and all insignia. As an exception, headgear, gloves, and handbags may be recovered when in the best interest of the Government and when directed by HQDA (see this regulation).

Personnel
The terms personnel, military personnel, service member, and civilian employee mean DA members, ARNG members or technicians, or DA civilian employees, unless otherwise stated.

Reserve Officer Training Corps and/or Simultaneous Membership Program
A voluntary officer status for eligibility. The program permits eligible enlisted personnel assigned to a TPU of the USAR to enter the advanced MS I and IV course of the ROTC Program. It also permits eligible ROTC advanced course cadets to be assigned to a TPU and serve as officer trainees.

Service uniform
A uniform prescribed for wear by Army personnel on routine duty. Different from dress, utility, or field combat uniforms.

State
Includes the 50 States, Commonwealth of Puerto Rico, territory of the U.S. Virgin Islands, territory of Guam, and the District of Columbia.

Supplemental allowances
Items and quantities of personal clothing authorized for issue to enlisted members to supplement initial allowances. They are given to persons whose assigned duties require more quantities of items than are included in initial issues. Is also given to those whose assigned duty that requires special items of personal clothing not normally issued to the majority of enlisted members.

Unit commanders
Commanders of companies, batteries, or similar units, and correctional officers.

U.S. property and fiscal officer
A commissioned officer of the Army or National Guard of the United States on extended Federal active duty and who is accountable and responsible for proper obligation and expenditure of all Federal funds and for receipt and account all Federal property in possession of the National Guard of the State; maintains an stock record account comparable to the level of a CONUS installation; and must ensure that accountability for Federal property is maintained after property is issued to property book level.

Section III
Special Abbreviations and Terms

USDEL
United States Delegation

Made in the USA
Columbia, SC
17 December 2022